Is there a God?
Hell, Yeah!

THE JODI FAITH STORY, LOL!

BY JODI FAITH
AS TOLD TO CHARLOTTE REED

 **FriesenPress**

Suite 300 – 990 Fort Street
Victoria, BC, Canada V8V 3K2
www.friesenpress.com

Copyright © 2014 by Jodi Faith
First Edition — 2014

ISBN
978-1-4602-4837-9 (Hardcover)
978-1-4602-4838-6 (Paperback)
978-1-4602-4839-3 (eBook)

1. Religion, Christian Life, Personal Growth

Distributed to the trade by The Ingram Book Company

TABLE OF CONTENTS

Dedications

Welcome to "The Jodi Faith Story, LOL!" I don't take it for granted that you decide to spend time with me here! I pray you'll consider it 'time well wasted!' LOL! Laugh Out Loud! A modern-day term used to describe "joy unspeakable!" Those "just made you chuckle! – Smile! – Celebrate with glee!" kind of moments! As I ponder my life and the remarkable ways my story has evolved, I "LOL" again and again! Over and over through these last few years of knowing Miss Charlotte, we have laughed together! That's where we must begin today!

I want to truly honor my writing partner, my "co-writer" and friend, Charlotte Reed. The first contact we had was when she emailed me. I was invited to a women's conference as the speaker and entertainer in the town where her aunt lived. Her concern was, and I quote, "I want to know who you are, what Jodi Faith is all about, what you'll be speaking on, and whether it will be worth my time and effort to attend or not!" LOL!! I truly had to "laugh out loud" at her bold questions and directness!

As I swallowed my smile, I called her. I told her the name of the conference was "Blossom!" All I was sure of at that precise moment was that I'd be discussing my experiences... and the fact that I'd overcome a whole lot of crap in my life! (Plowing through, trenching and working through all of it was truly empowering!) "After all", I said, "it can take a lot of 'bull s---'" to grow the best gardens!!" We immediately laughed together!

As our relationship began right there on the spot, we chatted like old friends. Charlotte shared some of the b.s. she'd been through in her life also and the fact that she was finishing a writing class. I responded out loud by saying, "You're a writer? Wow, that's awesome!" My husband, overhearing our conversation, said, "You should ask her if she wants to write your book!" And with that, dear friends, we partnered to bring you the rest of the story! LOL!

Charlotte could not have known how many times I had been asked for my story. Bob and I had prayed about God opening the door for my story to be written and suddenly Charlotte comes into our lives! We decided we really could do this thing together. A voice recorder was purchased, many phones calls and visits took place, Charlotte asked the pertinent questions and, as I shared, the words of the story began to flow. Sometimes I struggled with the way Charlotte stated what I'd said... "Seems like it's so formal and well spoken" I thought. Then one day she reminded me, in that direct approach I've so come to admire, "Well, Jodi, you really don't have great grammar and spelling at times you know!" LOL!!

What a blessing she has been in our lives! What a wonderful gift she remains! J<><

A word from Charlotte...

Meeting and seeing Jodi Faith perform today, you would have no idea that her past was difficult, painful and full of fear. I'd say I now know that through it all, God was with her and took her from that very dark place and transformed her life.

In writing this book she doesn't want the world to hear her story from a "soap box" perspective, but rather in a way that lives may be changed by it. It's her simple story – take it or leave it. That may not be the way business is done, but it is how ministry is done. Just to have another autobiography written about someone important isn't what this book is about. It is about telling the story of a living God who has proven Himself faithful, loyal and trustworthy to a simple girl who feels humbled and yet highly favored. It's a story about a God who pursued a quiet, broken sparrow with His love and showed her He'd loved her since before time began. A story about a God who has valued her and lifted her up, out of the mess she'd made of her life, to bless her with peace and joy, mercy and hope... A story worthy of being told... A story worthy of belief.

Jodi is working on decorating my kitchen while we worked on the book. The backsplash had been removed leaving a scarred surface that had never been restored and so after she arrived she thought it should be done. That is the interior decorator inside her. As she works and talks, she was so intent on fixing the backsplash that she grabbed and was talking into the 'square' rather than the voice recorder. It was only one of the many moments shared, "laughing out loud" together during the process of getting this story into print.

Being part of getting the Jodi Faith story into writing has literally changed my life! God brought together two women who had been through a lot of in their lives. He had restored them to wholeness and the result was a relationship like nothing I could have imagined. We clicked on every level and within a short time became family. The statement Bob and Jodi make that "your misery will become your ministry" struck me early on and it has been interesting to see God working to that end. One thing with this couple is that you will not find a more genuine desire to love and serve. Their home and lives are open books and Christ is seen and exemplified in their daily lives....they live their faith moment by moment! There is nothing God would ever ask them to do which they would say is too hard. It just means being completely surrendered to the one true God and letting Him have control.

As Jodi says, we all have a story to tell...be bold and share what God is doing in your life today! Become men and women of destiny! It is Jodi's prayer that I'll receive many more opportunities to write the stories of others whom God has called to share their lives with the world! It is the answer to Jodi's prayers that this project even came to be.

Charlotte Reed
306-920-7733
Email: reed.charlotte@hotmail.com
Writer-At-Large/Freelancer

A word from Jodi…

To my immensely loving and gracious family, my blessed and beautiful children, stepchildren, their significant others and our glorious grandchildren – God only knows how much I love and appreciate each of you and your remarkable uniqueness, gifts and talents. I love you deeply and thank God for each one of you! The ministry I have had has kept me away from you as many as 325 days a year and my sacrifice has been yours also. I thank you for your understanding and encouragement. In the end, the hardest part of writing this story is the fact that it isn't just my story to tell! I ask forgiveness from anyone who feels offended by these writings. I hope you know that was never, ever my intention.

My mom and I were chatting on the phone a while back and laughing so hard together. We've always had that – the laughter thing. It's been so good sometimes and my favorite part of my relationship with her; the "laugh until you cry" kind of mirth we have been able to share!

I was telling her how hard this book thing has been and finally just blurted out, "And Mom, it's supposed to be called 'The Jodi Faith Story – Laugh Out Loud!'" And she said, "Yes?" And I said, "And it's just not even funny!" And we both burst out laughing! With tears streaming down my face some of the tension seemed to let go and then my mom gave me another one of those remarkable tidbits of wisdom she's always been pulling out of her hat! She said, "Well, you could always change the name of the book!" I was almost rolling on the floor again! Sooooo perfect.

My Oma gave me permission during ministry events, to tell my version of her life and our relationship. I love the idea that she just might be watching, looking down on us from heaven as we testify to her amazing influence in my life. What a gift from God it was to have had a woman like her in my life. Interestingly, some people have questioned things she told me that she never told anyone else. From others, I've learned circumstances might have been different than I remember her telling me! Bottom-line, I sometimes wish it were a simpler time and I could live across town or just down the road from my grandchildren, too! I know the truth of how important a grandma/granddaughter relationship can be. I pray I will be allowed to be a mentor, hero and friend to my grandchildren, just as she was to me!

My story continues to be one of those "ordinary creatures living an extraordinary life" kind of stories – far from perfect, an old clay pot am I and close to cracking a lot of the time, but thank goodness, His mercy is new every Tuesday, right? LOL!! NO! The appropriate answer is God's mercy is new every morning. I have learned, too, that His grace and favor do not depend on my reaching some almost unattainable breatharian status or getting all my chakras in a row. Thank you, Jesus!

Considering there were many years when I tried to escape and ignore the existence of God in my life, He continued to pursue me, fill me, lead me and use me. Most wonderfully, it has been astounding to be reminded of how He revealed himself to me and to hear of the ways God Himself touched people through me. At the same time, it is very humbling too hear how the words I spoke or songs I sang inspired others, extended hope or joy and, in some cases, literally changed peoples' lives!

This book is sincerely dedicated to each person who has ever sown into
the life and ministry Bob and I have!
To the many faithful friends who have supported
us through prayer and financial support!
To Charlotte Reed for helping these words find life!
To Jacqueline Chartrand for pushing the project to the finish line!
To Marie Idler for her desire to hear the story
and for her proofreading efforts!

This book is dedicated also:
To the people of my childhood and my misspent youth,
for whom I continue to pray!
To the people God has ministered to through me.
Thank you for allowing me to serve you
and to grow as a minister. As a broken old clay pot,
restored and blessed beyond belief
by the one true living God; the Father, Son and Holy Spirit;
The Alpha and Omega,
I am who I am today because God knew I would know you!

This book seeks to honor each and everyone who is called to the frontline!
To the many leaders and ministers who have extended
God's love and wisdom toward me!
To Robert Faith – you have loved me and encouraged me
to have a voice and share from the heart.
You have propelled this ministry forward in spite of all it has cost you.
We have been dangerous for the Kingdom of God together and I thank you.
It is no wonder the enemy wants to destroy us!
Thank you for remaining committed to fight the
good fight as a frontline warrior with me!

Finally, to each of you, who have taken the time to read this story! Thank you!
Although God is obviously not finished with me yet, this book is my way
of celebrating how He has
brought me to a place of truth and transparency, able to
simply share my life and journey with you! J<><

Is there a God?
Hell, Yeah!

THE JODI FAITH STORY, LOL!

International Recording Artist and Media Personality,
Jodi Faith,
Shares her "Journey of Discovery" with
co-writer, Ms Charlotte Reed

www.bobandjodifaith.com
www.sonicbids.com/jodifaith
www.xpmedia.com/channel/bobandjodifaith

WHAT IN THE WORLD ARE YOU DOING WITH ME, AND TO ME, AND THROUGH ME, LORD?! J<><

Standing backstage, having just received the "5 minutes to walk on" cue, I am experiencing butterflies in my belly for the first time in years! Chuckling to myself I think, "Wow! Look how far you've come, girlfriend!! Uh, huh!" Laughing out loud in a slightly breathy chuckle, I knew I could be a bit too loud if I wasn't careful. A kind of giddiness was threatening to explode and I was smiling from ear to ear, too! "Thank you Jesus! What an adventure!"

Linda Cross, the President for US operations of the Vision Heaven Television Studio, had warned me it would be an awesome, but crazy, busy ride. I couldn't help but agree! It really was amazing! From the prairies of Saskatchewan, Canada to Mesa, Arizona in order to escape the Canadian winter, to this! Performing one of my own tunes in front of an estimated million-plus viewers in Scandinavia tonight and who knows where else in the great big beautiful world…

Awesome and humbling, and oh, my goodness! Suddenly I tear up, feeling overwhelmed by the opportunity and the reality of my amazing life. If I hadn't been willing to sing country music, my rendition of ***Random Acts of Kindness*** by friend and mentor, Russ Scherer, wouldn't have been at #1 for 32 weeks in 50 nations of the world. I used to say I hated country music and would apologize for singing it in concert almost every time, but my jingle, ***Lady of Destiny*** has been played in over 50 countries, too, and was at #1 for 16 weeks consecutively. My "Christian Country" songs had been playing in Norway for years. Without that specific credibility, I suddenly realized as I stood there watching fingers counting down, I probably wouldn't have been invited to be a part of this amazing event! So, not my plan but God's!! Most important moment of my life and I knew my make-up was getting messed up, really? As the tears flowed down my cheeks I got the sign to head upstage, swallowed and, with a quivering lip worked to smile. I prepared to walk into the spotlight. I would sing from a heart overflowing with gratitude and love for the Lord God Almighty, Who had never given up on me but had been there beside me through thick and thin.

Three, two, one… Live! I step into center stage and begin to share my thoughts as the intro to the song begins…

To a thousand generations… Please God, let me be an inspiration to my children, grandchildren, great grandchildren… J<><

My paternal Grandma, Maria (Mary) Peters Heidebrecht, whom I always called Oma, was a special person in my life and meant the world to me. I hold such fond memories of my Oma and love her dearly. Often during engagements, I will share insights I received from my Oma. A bond was formed between us that I never felt with anyone else. This bond was strengthened as a young child by my biweekly visits as I spent every Wednesday evening and Saturday night at Oma's house. I'd go to Oma's place so my parents could have time alone together. Memories of plain red Jell-o and rocking chairs, baking, bedtime snacks and bath time with favorite old toys fill my heart with warmth even now. Playing with the pedal on Oma's treadle sewing machine – a precious pastime! Auntie Katie and Auntie Helen, my dad's younger sisters, had me singing and performing for Oma during those early years; a tradition that would grow and continue. Family and Christmas gatherings always meant impromptu performances by all the cousins, with the adults listening and applauding generously or finally singing along in beautiful harmony. Smiling as I reminisce and share with Charlotte, I just have to add, "That's Mennonite harmony!"

As a teenager visiting Oma's home… on family holidays and then as a young mom myself, I spent many hours of quality time with my precious Oma. A special season in my life was when Oma would visit, arriving on the bus, to help me out with my young family. Babysitting and helping with my busy household, often cleaning, doing laundry or baking, Oma would share her stories of life, stories of the old country: what it was like

1

to live in the Mennonite village where she'd grown up in Russia, and how difficult it was when the war came and the men were taken away. Oma's father, the preacher, was suddenly gone and so many brothers, never to be seen again!

Loaded onto a train, leaving everything behind, the women and children followed the men to Poland. Oma had simply wanted to die when her beloved husband was killed after being conscripted into the German army. A conscientious objector, my grandfather and his kind were used as mine-sweeps ahead of the troops. A sad, short-lived tour of duty, he was dead a full year before Oma knew it to be true. How hard it had been for her, being a widow in a foreign land! She said she was literally unable to get out of bed for days after she got the news. Oma spoke often of her mother and grandmother, of their determination, strength and stamina, of their contributions to her children's lives and their home. Together, they had refused to let the young widow give in to the depression and hopelessness that overtook her at the thought of being alone as a young mother. Oma said she would never have survived that time… never made it to Canada without their perseverance and resolve.

There would be times in my life when I would remember the determination of these women and would be empowered by the memory of their tenacity to survive against all odds. Today, I love to sing *An Eagle When She Flies* by Dolly Parton and dedicate it to the amazing women we have had the honor to know… heroes… mentors… friends!

> *Gentle as a sweet magnolia…*
> *Strong as steel her faith and pride*
> *She's an everlasting shoulder…*
> *She's the leaning post in life*
> *She hurts deep and when she weeps,*
> *She's just as fragile as a child*
> *She's a sparrow when she's broken,*
> *But she's an eagle when she flies!*

At times, Oma would share almost nonchalantly about the journey to safety across the war-torn lands of Europe, and the challenges of working to support her three children, mother and grandmother. She would also share her story of securing passage and the journey across the sea to

Canada to finally settle in Coaldale, Alberta. Having become a born-again Christian she then learned to trust in God's genuine concern for her and her family. She began to build a heritage of faith for her family. As she shared her stories, she was always so proud to remind me of how her sacrificial determination to build a life for her family in Canada had led to the wonderfully blessed and successful lives her brother and children and their children were all now living.

During a visit in 1994, all hell broke loose and I was truly scared for my life. As a newly single mom, I was wondering what the future might hold. As I shared my fears, suddenly Oma spoke sternly. "Jodi, you've always known of God's plan for your life and you mustn't give up!" She shared how she had seen the pain in my eyes and had known of the sadness of my life for a long time. As she would pray about these things, Oma said she was often reminded of how God had shown her His plans for my life and she would claim those promises. On that fateful day, Oma shared how, in 1961, she was told she was going to be a grandmother. Engaged, but not yet married, her son was to be a father. This was a big deal back in the day and especially in the conservative religious community they were a part of. Oma spoke of the scandal it might have been. The elders of her church actually approached such issues with condemnation and judgment and advised Oma that this baby, who represented sin, must be shunned.

As Oma told me the story, her eyes welled up with tears of compassion and unconditional love. Holding my hand, she said she had prayed and asked God what she should do about this. Oma told me how God's peace had filled her and how He had reminded her in Psalm 139 that He had knitted this baby together in the womb and that He had plans and purposes for this child. For me! He knew my name and the number of hairs on my head! My heart was blessed with hope and inspiration for my future as Oma and I agreed in prayer that God's plans would be fulfilled for my seemingly broken, hopeless life.

As I remember my paternal grandmother and honor her, as I speak of her and the legacy she left behind, I ask God to let me be to mine what she has been to ours! **God, your God, has multiplied your numbers. Why, look at you—you rival the stars in the sky! And may God, the God-of-Your-Fathers, keep it up and multiply you another thousand times, bless you just as he promised.** (Deuteronomy. 1:11)

HONOR YOUR MOTHER AND FATHER... SO THAT IT'LL GO
WELL WITH YOU! A BLESSING WITH A PROMISE! J<><

My parents, Henry (nicknamed Heidi) Heidebrecht and Cheryl-Ann
Livingston, were married on April 1ˢᵗ, 1961. Oma recalled the way the
wind sent my mom's veil straight up into the air and how she'd felt a good
bit of anxiety and concern for the possible storms this young couple would
have in their marriage. My mom was "from money" and from the city and
as Oma told it, she was very strong-willed, too! And Heidi, her eldest and
only son, was very spoiled and rebellious as well! Oh my, she'd sometimes
laugh when she talked about them and how she'd worried! She said she
determined right then and there on that crazy, windy wedding day to
pray for them as much as she possibly could! Laughing, she'd admitted to
praying for them almost constantly in those early days!

My mom recalled meeting her future mother-in-law for the first time
on a street corner where Oma was passing out gospel tracts. Mom admits
that she didn't know quite what to think of her boyfriend's old-fashioned
and obviously Mennonite mother! She was so kind and sweet, but giving
out religious materials? Oh, my! That same evangelistic spirit would be
passed on to Oma's firstborn granddaughter. My mom related how I, as
a little girl of three, returned from church with Oma one Sunday and
immediately asked, "Daddy, where are you going to go when YOU die?"
Mom said it was not very long before she and dad were also saved. In
1976, my dad took up that same spirit of concern for the spiritual condition of men, women and children and became a member of the Gideon's
International organization. Distributing Bibles locally and abroad with
the ministry, he was joined by my mom just a few years later. A wonderful
time for Bob and me is hearing the stories my folks tell of how people

react to the free gift of Bibles offered as they travel the world. After our marriage, we became members of this worthwhile organization, excited to be in ministry together. Since that time, my brother and sister and their spouses have taken up membership as well.

I have wonderful memories of the annual holiday our family enjoyed in Penticton, BC each summer. I remember my dad getting doused by mom with ice cold river water every year and Oma laughing so hard, tears streamed down her face! "Henry!" Oma would say, with exasperation! LOL!! An always wonderful time of camping and swimming with our daddy who became the famous and legendary Ogopogo!

Lots of fun with family swimming nights and winter downhill skiing; visits with favorite cousins, family gatherings, summer picnics and trips to the farm in Coutts with mom's parents, Grandma (Belle) and Papa (Clarence) Livingston. I loved the great big, exciting family birthday parties (as all three of us Heidebrecht kids had birthdays within a month of each other). I will never forget my mom's most delicious and beautifully decorated character birthday cakes – such an awesome surprise each year! My personal favorite is still the "elephant!"

Looking back, I also had to deal with some less than pleasant memories and a few crazy and funny moments from the old neighborhood. I crawled into mommy and daddy's bed one winter morning to see daddy's great big swollen lip and the many stitches he'd received the night before during his recreation hockey game (my dad was an amazing player and probably could've been in the NHL if he'd had the money to get noticed!). Then across the street, there was the lady who made and decorated the most beautiful cakes I have ever seen. They sat under a lovely glass bubble on her counter and NO ONE ever got to taste them. I had been told, "Silly child! They are only for looking at!"

I have memories of the nasty kids on my block being mean to one another. I became a bully myself and part of the wicked pack mentality that runs rampant among kids surviving the summer heat. I repented of that not long ago actually!! I also remember running home to avoid having to play "doctor" with creepy kids whose names I no longer recall.

I grew up in a home where we said "I'm sorry" and "I love you!" There is a wonderful verse in the Bible that says, **"Honor your father and your mother, as the LORD your God has commanded you, so that you will**

live long and that it may go well with you in the land the LORD your God is giving you." (Deuteronomy 5:16) I realize they shared a beautiful and deep commitment towards one another and to our family. Throughout all these years I have chosen to honor spirit of dedication and loyalty they modeled. My dad was a well respected employee and worked hard at the same company until venturing out into his own business. My mom was a stern disciplinarian and kept the house well organized! While looking back, I must say I know I felt loved. I always felt secure growing up. I loved my siblings and life at home most of the time. A popular song on the radio, *D-i-v-o-r-c-e* was never something we ever heard threatened. I often think that was amazing because my parents did fight! I sometimes felt sorry for my dad because I thought my mom could be so demanding and really hard to live with at times. My main desire was to *not* rock the boat! The old adage, "if mama's not happy, nobody's happy" was how I felt! When I discovered at 12, that they had been pregnant with me when they got married, I felt so guilty. Was it my fault he'd been stuck with us?

At the same time I loved my mom! My mom was brilliant and made sure we got a break from the busyness and stresses of life by giving us the earliest bedtime known to children the world over! We still like to tease my mom about it! The neighborhood kids would sneak into the backyard to visit us through our basement bedroom window. Warm memories include my beloved new baby brother, Jason, a big blue-eyed gift from God, and my younger sister Renae. She and I had great fun playing circus in bed every night in the bedroom we shared. Using my feet to lift her high in the air, I'd accidentally send her into the wall and we'd hear dad pounding down the steps to threaten us with spankings if we didn't settle down! Playing school with my siblings and cousins was such a 'happy place' for me. I realized years later, being a primary school teacher was probably what I was created to do. Then there was the annual guessing game challenge of trying to decipher my mom's crazy codes on every unlabeled Christmas gift and *never* being able to guess even one correctly!

More memories;
Cocoa and toast and campfires, too... J<><

Although I assume it was all pretty much okay, I have only a few very specific memories of my first years of school. I recall having to walk over a mile or more every day to and from school. On a rare occasion I traveled with my dad, through what seemed to be mile-high snowdrifts on both sides of the vehicle. I also have a weird, scary, very vague recollection of a dark-hooded man in a black car in a back alley, which I have chosen to ignore and keep very deeply buried!

However, I'm willing to share quite openly two very specific, ridiculously embarrassing memories from grade two! Firstly, having to spell "TV" during the weekly spelling bee, I drew a complete blank and finally ended up spelling it t-e-e-v-e-e! Wrong! Oh, my! LOL! Secondly, I remember suffering the horrible humiliation of having to admit to stealing a chocolate egg from my teacher's desk. One by one, second graders lined up, trekked through the boot room and around to the front of the room, marching past that desk as the teacher waited for the egg to be returned! It was quite an ordeal for all of us. It couldn't be returned because I had eaten it! Arghhh! Putting an end to the drama, I finally admitted to my crime. Suffice it to say, I never stole anything *ever* again!! What a lesson well learned! LOL!

I was 'saved' at Camp Evergreen in Sundre, Alberta at only six years old. I was 'born-again!' A memory I still hold dear. I had been attending church regularly with my Oma and later with my parents, and even at such a young age, I had a deep spiritual awareness. Discovering that I could live forever in Heaven and not burn in hell filled my heart with hope. I remember my mom being there as a wonderful part of that moment.

Camp was always such a beautifully refreshing and restorative time each summer! Getting worn down and somewhat lukewarm in my spiritual consciousness, I would get filled back up every year at camp. My favorite times were around the campfire each night and the songs we'd all sing together. *He's Everything To Me* was my favorite and still resonates deeply in my grateful heart. It can be found on the TRIBUTE album

> *In the stars His handiwork I see*
> *On the wind He speaks with majesty*
> *Though He ruleth over land and sea*
> *What is that to me?*
> *Til by faith I met Him face to face*
> *And I felt the wonders of His grace*
> *Then I knew that he was more than just a God who didn't care*
> *Who lives away up there*
> *And now He walks beside me day by day*
> *Ever watching o'er me lest I stray*
> *Helping me to find the narrow way*
> *He's everything to me!*

Although camp was always a great and wonderful experience, getting back into the Sunday School and "Church" world each fall was almost always a huge letdown. At camp I learned I was to help change the world with God's love. I always came back so excited to be a part of the solution but would be bullied and become a bully at church instead. Brutal, but true! In hindsight I've learned that was yet another reason why I probably ended up going down the broken road. I've come to terms with the fact that I had very low self-esteem even as a young child, so looking for validation from friends at church was natural. One of the girls would announce each week that we were not to "talk" to this girl or that! Becoming one of the bullies in order to *not* rock the boat is another of the deep regrets I have had to forgive myself for. I have had to claim the great promise from scripture, **"His mercy is new every morning!"** (Lamentations 3:22-23 – NIV). Ironically, I thought if I played the nasty role it would keep me from being picked on. You could cut through the tension like butter on those days when the edict had gone out and the clique was *not* speaking to me! Better memories include Pioneer Girls Club on Wednesday nights, which was pretty cool, although my most vibrant memories of it were eating rice with our fingers during "India Missionary" moments, LOL!! Another wonderful memory I have of church in those years includes getting notes in my jacket pocket from the boy who liked me.

A super cool memory I have of third grade is being selected to sing and represent my school at music festival. I remember practicing hard to learn *A Goblin Went A-Hiking On A King's Highway.* I remember wondering how in the world the adjudicator would ever be able to pick a first and second place winner! I love remembering, too my dad's crazy little comment, "Oh, my shattered nerves!" after listening to 32 versions sung badly or well of that exact song! He said he wasn't even sure it mattered who won anymore! Imagine our surprise as I received first place and the wonderful kudos from a voice teacher, who came out of the crowd to ask if I would become her student. Mrs. Ellen Mells became a wonderful mentor who taught me Royal Conservatory Voice lessons. She helped me prepare for Kiwanis Music Festivals each year and guided me to many awards over a ten year period.

Mom and dad, I will be forever grateful for the huge sacrifices you made in allowing me those lessons! I thank you for the opportunity! Thanks for driving me back and forth, for the sacrifice of finances and time and the huge effort of listening to and critiquing my songs. I dedicate my version of ABBA's *I Have A Dream* to you both!

I have a dream, a fantasy, to help me through reality
And my destination makes it worth the while
Pushing through the darkness still another mile
I believe in angels, something good in everything I see
I believe in angels, and when I know the time is right for me
I'll cross the stream, I have a dream

Surely a dream was born in me as Dad and I sang along. For years, ABBA was played on the 8-track player on those weekly trips to the city! "Thanks, mom, for listening and constructively criticizing everything from Irish love songs to Italian selections year after year!" Even while visiting just recently, mom was once more willingly listening to and critiquing my rendition of *Danny Boy* for our Patriotic Pageant in Mesa, AZ.

Talking about my mom reminds me of her amazing butter horns and homemade cocoa and toast, crabapple jelly and lunch boxes to be proud of! Back-to-school always began with fabulous shopping expeditions to Great Falls, Montana! Then, there was fourth grade and my first male teacher (very cute Mr. Ackerman), who introduced us to a really cool open concept learning environment where there were no desks, only tables and centers! I thought it was awesome and amazing! I loved, loved, LOVED to sing and have fun memories of being a part of "The Happy Wanderers" in fifth grade after we moved to Coaldale from Lethbridge. I recall being one of two new students in class and the scary teacher I had, who had a big cardboard box in the back of the room where you'd have to go sit, all alone, if you were ever bad! Another memory is of the shocking morning at school when we learned that the other new student and his dad had been killed as they crossed the train tracks. Sadly, the school didn't offer counseling for such things back then. I can pinpoint that time as when a fear of death at any moment began to brood deep within my spirit.

Music was always a solace to me. My music lessons and vocal training were a wonderful blessing and I excelled in my festival entries with first or second place awards in every class I entered year after year. The only bad mark I ever got was actually in German because the adjudicator had looked at my last name (Heidebrecht) and assumed I could speak German. He suggested my poor diction was because I was being lazy in my enunciation! He assumed wrongly, however, as I had never spoken more than a simple one line prayer in German!

I remember singing special musical numbers in church throughout the years and participating briefly in a kid's choir there as well. A special memory throughout my youth was singing for my maternal grandparents. My Grandma and Papa Livingston always asked for a song at every visit! They even paid for my cousin Dixie and me to cut a record. It was a pretty cool experience! They wanted us to perform **Put On Your Old Grey Bonnet** for the one side of the 45, while we could choose any other song we liked for the other side. We chose Jim Croce's **If I Could Save Time In A Bottle**. I remember Dixie having to play the songs over and over on the piano before getting the recording right. A short time later, my parents received a call from the recording studio in New York City who were producing and manufacturing our little 45. Apparently, they offered me a recording

IS THERE A GOD? HELL, YEAH!

deal and said, "Your daughter could be the next Tanya Tucker!", to which my parents said, "No, thanks!" I recognize that this was a turning point in my life as I gave up on my hidden heart's desire to be a singer when I grew up! Having no a clear vision for my future left me in a very vulnerable place.

THANKS FOR NOT GIVING UP ON ME THOUGH I WENT THE WRONG WAY! J<><

It's with detached curiosity that I now analyze how I ended up in such a mess of drug and alcohol abuse and the domestic violence that is part of the Jodi Faith story.

I can't help but remember a moment of deep significance at about 12 years of age. I very distinctly remember the sermon the pastor preached one Sunday morning in church. Everything I'd just learned at summer camp was reiterated as he said, "We Christians are the only example of God's love that people are going to see in the world! Together, we can change the world by going out the doors of the church and showing love to friends and neighbors and strangers alike!"

I wanted so much to be a part of that change! I hoped all my Sunday school friends were listening, too! No more being mean to anyone, only goodness and kindness! As the organist sent us out with a great song, we went off to change the world!! It was traditional to file out of the church in an orderly fashion from the front rows to the back. The pastor would step off the platform and head down the center aisle ahead of the crowd in order to be standing ready at the back of the church, where he would greet each of us with a warm handshake. The young people sitting at the front of the church followed behind him exiting one row at a time. I was right behind the preacher and felt very excited to shake his hand in support of his great message.

Obviously not aware of the exit strategy, standing up and entering the center aisle just ahead of me was a long-haired hippie-looking visitor. (The church was located just off a main road into the city, easily accessible for travelers to attend.) I saw the visitor reach out to shake the preacher's hand. Then I watched in disbelief as my pastor put his hand behind his back and ignored the man, not shaking hands or acknowledging the stranger at all! As the stranger walked ahead, the pastor reached for my hand! Instead of feeling like a blessing had been extended toward me, anger and bitterness took root even deeper in my heart as the word "hypocrite!" screamed loudly from my soul.

Growing up Mennonite Brethren meant I wasn't allowed to smoke, drink or dance. However, the Mennonite Conference people smoked, drank and danced. I always wondered why we couldn't just change churches and become Mennonite Conference because it would be so much better. This all became a huge issue for me after we moved to Coaldale and the junior high school offered school dances. I was told by my parents that I wouldn't be allowed to participate. Discussing it at great length, they told me that there wasn't necessarily anything wrong with dances, but rather it was the behavior that went along with the dancing that was so bad. All this did for me was whet my appetite for whatever that behavior was.

Although I believe it really is a long journey that leads to rebellion, my attitude of disrespect had grown towards the Christian culture I lived in. I felt it was completely controlled by hypocrites. Pastors couldn't be trusted, adults gossiped about families within the church over Sunday dinners and the kids all treated each other horribly! Huge generalizations for sure, but I know without a doubt by this time I was done with all of them and began looking for friends in all of the wrong places.

In the seventh grade, a girlfriend invited me to an overnight sleepover; my very first sleepover with a friend from school. Her older brother was having a party and we began to drink vodka and orange juice. I ended up drunk and threw up all night long. Of course, this became a huge secret; neither of us wanting my parents to find out. Then smoking became the next secret sin, during lunch hours or after school, bumming smokes from friends. There was something in me that wanted that sort of thing in my life even at such a young age. My Christian upbringing caused feelings of deep guilt because of these secrets. I remember absolutely hating having to go to church, thinking I couldn't wait to get out on my own and do what I wanted to do.... no rules attached! Rebellion led me to make decisions that were unhealthy.

As so many young girls, I wanted a boyfriend! I felt I'd prove myself accepted and validated if I just had a boyfriend. There were always a couple of boys at church I was attracted to and a few fellows at school that I was head over heels in love with. Spending time with these boys and friends was so important I remember almost breaking my Oma's heart by staying out way past curfew one evening. Jason, Renae and I were staying with her while my parents were on their first overseas holiday to Germany. Oma was devastated when I finally got home! She just couldn't understand why I'd do something like this to her; after all, we both loved and respected each other so much! There was no way Oma could comprehend why I'd choose to be so bad. That night I lay in bed and wondered as well.

Being bullied in Sunday School, becoming a bully there and floundering as I determined that "church" would no longer be part of my life, led to a greater need of being validated by having friends. I was even willing to jeopardize my relationship with Oma to sneak out and stay out late. Now I know a spirit of rebellion was rising up in me. It started to destroy my life at 12 and 13 years of age as I began to struggle with respect for the things my parents had taught me. This rebellion is prevalent at even younger ages today. In my teaching ministry, I really emphasize that we need to bring that rebellious spirit into the light and rebuke it in Jesus' name

Just a few years later, my dad bought a business and our family moved to Brooks, Alberta. This was a pivotal time in my life. I had just finished the ninth grade and lived my entire life in the Lethbridge area. I'd grown up in the midst of a secure family network. My maternal and paternal grandparents and the extended family included many much-loved cousins. Family gatherings were common and I knew I was going to miss them all. It was a time of both excitement and trepidation as I pondered what was to come.

"WHO DO I WANT TO BE WHEN I GROW UP?" I ASKED,
WALKING DOWN THE BACK ALLEY AND
BLOWING PERFECT SMOKE RINGS! J<><

Leaving all these things behind, my greatest fear was meeting new friends.
I was going into grade ten, but school wouldn't start for a few weeks and
I thought I'd be lonely until then. As I was walking down the street one
day, a good-looking young guy drove up beside me in a really cool car
and said, "Hey, I don't know you." Introducing ourselves, he invited me
to a party that night. I was nervous as to how I would get permission to
go. I really wanted to go. I told my parents that I'd met this nice guy who
said a bunch of kids from school were going to be getting together. He
wanted me to come meet them all. They let me go and I felt welcomed so
completely into this new group that it was a wonderful relief.

The move to Brooks included leaving the church I'd attended my
whole life in Lethbridge. I didn't hold out much hope that things would
be great in any new church, but finding one was on the top of my parent's
list of things to accomplish as we settled into our new community. I still
remember the Sunday School teacher on my first Sunday there saying to
the other students, "Now I really want to ask you to be a friend to Jodi.
This must be really hard for her to have moved here, to go to high school
and have no friends. We are really excited to have somebody new in our
class and I'm asking you to be kind to her." With the exception of a couple
of the geeky guys, no one even made eye contact with me! After a few
weeks of attending, I knew I wasn't going to be friends with any of them.

Within days of school starting, I would walk down the hallways and
recognize these kids, but felt they would literally look the other direction and walk away. Sometimes, although they weren't even engaged in

conversations, I felt they'd do all they could to avoid me. I actually remember thinking, "You bunch of hypocrites!" and developed a nasty attitude toward these Christian kids, especially because their super nice Sunday School teacher had asked them to be nice to me. There were a couple of boys that tried to be nice to me, but none of the girls.

From an adult perspective, I might say they were probably shy, insecure or apprehensive themselves, but at that point in my life, once again I was offended by their behavior and felt invalidated. Even though this church should have been a safe place to go and spend time with kids, I soon developed the rebellious attitude that said, "Come hell or high water, there's no way I am going near these people or being friends with them."

In contrast, I remembered the sweet guy who had been so welcoming and how he'd offered to pick me up and take me to the party. All the new friends I'd met there seemed to go out of their way to be nice to me. Walking to school my first day, I met another girl who was also new to the area. Her dad had been transferred to Brooks. Not at all involved in the church community, she and I became fast friends. We would walk back and forth to school together, stopping to have a smoke and a pop at the local restaurant each day on our way home.

The desire to be part of the partying crowd had already begun and so I began to tell my parents about the great friends I was meeting and enjoying spending time with. My parents' idea of keeping me safe and out of trouble was giving me an early curfew. My mom was also as tenacious as a bulldog and wouldn't go to sleep at night until her kids were all home safe because she was concerned for us. She also expected to have a conversation with us when we got home. One thing I discovered very early was that if there was alcohol on my breath when I walked through the door, my mom could smell it a mile away. Having figured this out within a couple of weeks of going out with these new friends in Brooks, I started using marijuana because its' scent wasn't detectable to my mom. One of the times I walked in the door, my mom asked what was wrong since my eyes were so red. I told her that I'd been crying. This was the start of my lying. It was a new story every time, there had been a fight among the girls or the bonfire was smoky or some other such thing to explain why my eyes were red. I was also smoking at this time. Since mostly everyone in the group smoked, it was easy to blame them for the smoke mom could always smell on my clothes. When my mom asked if I was smoking, I told her, "Of course not!" More lying!

I never played around with anything more than hash and marijuana, which I felt were relatively safe and gentle drugs. With that entire group of friends, what we did was smoke, drink and 'do' pot together. The welcome and sense of belonging I felt for the first time in my life were exactly what I needed and enjoyed, and I felt like this was where I belonged. Over the next year and a half, I smoked pot pretty regularly. I began smoking up in the morning before I went to classes, skipping classes to go smoke up or getting loaded with friends after school. Ironically, I was usually sobered right up before my folks ever got home from work so they never had any idea what I was up to.

Today I also realize that everything in those days was about peer pressure, my friends and my validation from them because I didn't like myself. I didn't have good self-esteem and didn't think I was good-looking. I had always thought my sister was so cute and so tiny. My cousins were all skinny, too! I always felt like the ugly duckling, chunky, freckled and far from beautiful.

Immersed in the weekend party scene, I felt like I was part of the popular crowd of kids at school and at times definitely had some really cute guys interested in me. They wanted to spend time with me! Hoping for a "forever" boyfriend, flirting and necking and petting were all part of the scene. Loaded and under the influence of pot, I found myself in a few dangerous situations with these boys, even in a bedroom at a party with some guy I thought was a friend. Time and time again, I felt lucky to have escaped things getting out of hand. Although I played with fire, I can look back and admit that I was protected from being burned!

"Did you have sex!" Charlotte asked me straight out in her wonderfully forthright way. I was able to say I never had sex with any of the guys up to this point in time, partly because they often passed out before they could get the job done, which is entirely terrible, but true! Hard as I tried to live a conscience-free kind of life, I did find myself panicked and praying at those times! I grew up in a religious culture where you just didn't have premarital sex. Sex outside of marriage was wrong and was taboo. I knew if I was going to 'go all the way' and have sex with somebody, it had better be with the guy I was going to marry.

By the age of 15, I was convinced that if only I could meet the guy I was going to marry, then I could have sex and everything would be wonderful. Part of this likely stems from the fact that I'd been told my folks planned to get married, so getting pregnant beforehand was no big deal. They 'made it right' by getting married and creating a wonderful home for our family. Because it worked out so well for them, I believed being somebody's girlfriend, having sex and getting married would validate me. It became my sole purpose in living! This is obviously one of the biggest lies out there, especially for young girls. It is something Bob and I are hearing in schools and from youth everywhere that we now travel in ministry.

Whatever the reasons, I had the radar out for this special guy. Ironically, there was this really nice guy, Don, in my church who had been calling me. We had a couple of great conversations on the phone! I really liked him and thought he was genuinely nice. I was attracted to him and started getting to know his family since my parents wanted to know about him. I also learned he had an older brother who was known as the black sheep of the family. He'd run away from home at about 14 years of age. Something about his older brother's story appealed to that rebellious spirit within me.

My parents would give me an allowance to buy jeans or special things I wanted, but if I wanted designer clothes or more costly things I had to earn the money. I had a job at the Dairy Queen specifically for this purpose. I noticed this long-haired rough-looking guy who started showing up there. All I knew about him was that he ordered extra pickles on his burgers and I was really attracted to him. Even though he had the air of being a tough 'bad boy', I felt that he was so lonely. I would take my vinegar water and wash tables when he was there. It turned out that this was Don's older brother, Jim. Since Don was such a decent guy, I didn't have to be convinced that his brother was really a nice guy, too, underneath that tough exterior and hint of depression that was so often apparent.

After we had visited quite a number of times over his burgers and my cleaning, Jim finally asked me out. I was so excited! Although I already had plans to go to a huge party the next night, I accepted his invitation! We were going to the drive-in movie! I called my girlfriends, as girls do, all excited that I'd been asked out by Jim. They already knew I was somewhat interested in him because I'd talked about him so much. It was an easy choice to tell my friends that I was bailing out on them to go to the drive-in with him.

Old enough to know it's wrong, but young enough not to care!
Life is short and death ain't fair! J<><

At sixteen, in Grade eleven, I felt so-o-o grown up. I'd had a few boy-friends, but somehow this seemed different! I spent time getting ready and then he showed up at the door. His car was a huge, big old 'boat', some sort of classic car and something he obviously treasured because it was polished to the nth degree. I thought it was the ugliest thing I'd ever seen! He was dressed in western jeans with a huge belt buckle and cowboy boots. I was so disappointed and thought to myself, "Oh, brother! This is *so* not my kind of guy."

We went to the drive-in movie and started talking and he shared his story about how he had been rather harshly treated growing up. In his words, he had grown up in a conservative Mennonite environment. My heart broke for him as he shared how he had been brutally beaten by his parents and had never felt loved by anyone. I remember thinking, "It's awful that he never experienced a feeling of belonging or being part of the family."

Right from that first date, I thought, "If I could love him enough, I'll bet I could help him overcome all that loneliness and hurt!"

In hindsight, we all see life differently. Just as my siblings didn't have the life I had and my perception of what I saw differed greatly from the way they saw the situation, Jim Barg's life and story fit this scenario perfectly. I have edited about 3000 words from the telling of the 'Jim and me' tale because so much of it would have been his story to tell. Nonetheless, Jim talked all the way through the movie and we never watched any of the show. My heart was totally wrenched over the life he had lived. He spoke of how his family was 'born again' and how he had accepted the Lord at twelve years of age. When that happened, he thought his family and home were going to change so much. As Jim prayed the prayer of salvation to accept Jesus into his heart, he fully believed that his parents would change and that as kids, he and his three younger siblings would never get beaten again, and that the fighting and silent treatments would end. He believed that they would become a new family full of love and compassion. Yet the very next day he was beaten as badly or worse than he had ever been. Again, this was Jim's story and his perception of things. Whether it actually was that severe and whether he deserved the discipline or not, really is not known. It was the 1960's and 70's when corporal punishment was accepted as the method of child discipline.

By the end of that first night, I wondered how this could possibly have happened. This family had not only become 'born again' and the corporal punishment continued, but their religious community also shunned them. Jim's perception of this came from the fact that they had only been allowed to associate with people from their own religious community. That community had strict rules, such as no movie-watching. Therefore, in grade school, Jim and his little friends would have to sit out in the hall while the rest of the class watched a movie. After being 'born again', he said he walked back into the school full of his old "religious community" friends (that he had known since birth) and they all literally turned their backs on him. An edict had been sent out from their church that the kids were not allowed to speak to the Barg children anymore because they were no longer considered part of the community. All of this absolute isolation and devastation were put upon this young man, and all in the name of Jesus. So very harsh!

This was simply an old order Christian Mennonite community that was very conservative. Jim shared other stories with me about the first time his grandfather wore a tie in church and how he almost got booted out. In their church the girls sat on one side and the boys on the opposite side. One time the boys got some firecrackers and threw them over to the girls' side. Humorous, but basically they were just ordinary rebellious children. Church was attended Wednesday, Sunday morning and Sunday afternoons, and all of a sudden, they weren't allowed to be part of it anymore.

All of this was shared on that first night at the drive-in. I still remember thinking that all Jim needed was to be loved, that he had never been truly loved. I asked him, "You do know that God loves you though, don't you?"

"I don't really think that God does love me. No. If God truly loved me, He wouldn't have allowed my life to end up like it has," was Jim's reply. He shared how he always had wanted to farm and ranch and raise cattle. It had been his desire to be a veterinarian. Over a three-hour period, I heard his entire story.

I also recall that he drank a dozen or more beers during that double feature movie presentation. Innocent of such things in so many ways, I really didn't think anything of it at the time. As I think about it today, I realize there were signs even on that first night that I would be getting involved in a life I really didn't understand. There had never been any alcohol in my home while I was growing up, but Jim admitted to drinking since he was about eleven.

I felt that Jim was a wounded creature and that, if only I could show him some love, he would come around. He would realize he was valuable and that God loved him and would be able to fulfill his dreams. If only I could love him enough! So began my journey into the craziest and most codependent relationship a woman could ever lose herself in.

The morning after my first date with Jim Barg, I was sitting in church waiting for the service to begin. Behind me I heard two older ladies talking. One asked the other, "Did you hear about the hellions killed last night?" I was overwhelmed with grief as I heard the names of my girlfriends being reported. I sprang to my feet and ran out of the church and all the way home bawling like a baby. I realized my friends, whom I could have been with the night before, were gone! All my hurt and bewilderment became anger directed at those callous, hard-hearted women! I vowed I'd never go back! Hypocrites!

I ended up singing at some of those funerals. With the school choir I sang the Eagles' song, *Desperado*. That song still holds memories for me today. It spoke entirely to the whole idea that life sucks. I know I would never have rushed into a relationship with Jim Barg if circumstances had been different. If I hadn't gone out with him that night I, too, might have ended up dead. I became convinced that I didn't die that night because I was meant to be with him for whatever time I still had.

Late afternoon, on the day after they'd been killed, I gathered with friends to mourn the terrible deaths and tragic loss, when suddenly someone said, "They were all virgins, I think!" As I look back, I remember thinking that dying a virgin would be worse than death itself! Death might be inevitable, but not virginity! I made a pact to give up my virginity before it was too late!

The fear of getting pregnant was a big deterrent though because birth control products weren't easy to obtain. A teenaged girl could not even go to the doctor and get birth control pills without her mother's permission. If a girl did get pregnant, she just sort of had to disappear from home and society.

FOR BETTER OR WORSE? TO NOT LIVE HAPPILY EVER
AFTER, EVER? SERIOUSLY??
AS MEATLOAF HAD US CONVINCED, TWO
OUT OF THREE AIN'T BAD. J<><

During that summer of dating, Jim of course wanted to have sex. Scared as I was of dying a virgin, I told him that I wasn't allowed to have sex until I was engaged to be married. Jim asked me to marry him and we had sex. One of the interesting things that happened at this time is that I was able to find a doctor who would prescribe birth control pills. A huge secret that my mom had no idea about, it allowed me to start a very active sex life. Jim and I would spend literally hours and days in bed over each weekend. Life was all about sex, drinking and smoking pot together. Fighting between us was a regular thing, too. Jim tried to break up with me, but I fought desperately to stay engaged. He finally got me a ring and I felt somewhat more secure, but it was a strange time because I lived in constant fear of a break-up.

As unhealthy as the situation was, I realize today that I had bought into the biggest lie that would keep me in a relationship. I felt I was unworthy to ever be loved by anyone else since I had given myself to Jim. My virginity was gone and I was stuck! I felt I had sinned the unpardonable sin, having premarital sex! No matter what, we *had* to get married.

Being involved with someone four years older, I ended up leaving my circle of friends and my school community. I became quite isolated. I spent time partying with Jim and his friends to the extent that I dropped out of school in January of my grade twelve year. Jim and my dad both agreed that there would be no marriage until I graduated with my high school diploma. Working full-time in a bookkeeping job, I only needed two more credits, which I thought I could get through correspondence courses. I wasn't allowed to attend my high school graduation because, with work and partying, I had fallen behind the required time frame.

Jim and I went ahead and bought our first home in Brooks, Alberta and it overlooked the community centre where my entire graduation class was having our prom. I was so angry I wasn't allowed to attend, but I tried to convince myself it didn't matter. As I watched from behind the curtains, I saw all my old friends and classmates across the street celebrating and having a good time! I blamed the principal for his harsh ruling, rather than admit my failure to complete the required correspondence lessons on time.

When I talk to youth about how we destroy our destiny purposes, I am able to remind them that it really is God's will that they go to school. It is God's will that they are a part of a healthy school community. Today, Bob always says, "Don't limit your future options with short-sighted high school decisions!"

After a tumultuous engagement year when Jim tried to break up with me at least five times, I still did not believe I could possibly have a future without him. After partying costs, I didn't have much money either. I couldn't envision much of a future on my own even though I did have a daytime job. I was stuck.

Finally, the wedding plans began to take shape. No big beautiful wedding like every girl in the world dreams about, though. No! The original wedding invitations had been ordered for 200 people and the fruitcake had been made when Jim cancelled the spring wedding. I was experiencing so much fear and trepidation, I begged Jim for just a postponement and he finally relented. With the wedding planned for the following October, my Dad reminded me that I couldn't get married unless I graduated. I worked hard and got the correspondence course finished and received my diploma in the mail.

The invitations were recreated by burning the edges and center out of the originals. They were sent out. Jim got his way and only a quiet intimate group of twenty people were invited – just family. The only friend invited was Jim's best man and best friend. My sadness began to grow as I realized I didn't have any friends anymore. After talking to Art and Rachel Hildebrand, my pastor couple, about wedding plans, Jim was relieved to discover we would *not* be required to do any premarital counseling. Pastor Art had said he'd rather counsel us during the challenges to come after we were married! He was such a wise man! Although Jim was never willing to go for counseling, I often wondered during those first few years, if that would have been a help, if things might have been able to improve in our rocky world, if only we'd been willing to pick up the phone and ask.

I believe there were so many times when God was trying to slam the door on my relationship with Jim long before the wedding ever took place. I realize too though, that every time Jim tried to break up with me, I fought to stay in the relationship because I truly felt so unworthy of anyone else since I was no longer a virgin. In 1979, I married Jim Barg. I know my parents were concerned about me marrying him. After all, it had been a tough year. So often he would just not show up for dates and the reasons were just stupid; life wasn't easy. My parents could tell that things were not what they should have been, but they had also come to love this young man and wanted him to have a better life as well. On the morning of my wedding day, however, my dad told me, "You realize that just because things are tough doesn't mean you can come running home. If you go ahead with this, you are making a commitment to this relationship." I knew in my heart it had to be "until death do us part!"

A few months later my parents relocated from Brooks to Medicine Hat. I feel this is my dad's story to tell since his experience in Brooks didn't fare well and he ended up having to leave there out of a failed business partnership. My parents were totally devastated both personally and on a business level. When my marriage became hell on earth very quickly, I didn't want to burden them because they already had so much going on in their own lives. Due to the devastation that had taken place in his business relationship, my parents had literally watched their entire life in Brooks deteriorate. They ended up having to scramble and move out of town to have food on their table! It had been a brutal time for them and I had no interest in burdening them with what I knew was my mistake! I discovered years later, that my dad felt deep regret over his wedding day advice to me when he realized how horrible my life had been. He took deep responsibility for the fact that I stayed in that relationship although I never ever blamed him at all!

I had no idea that life could be as ugly as it was. My parents' situation and mine! We all had to endure so much more ugliness over the next few years. Such was life! In hindsight, I believe I would never have stayed in the marriage. I would have left and gone home if things hadn't been going so badly for my parents. Bottom line though, even this is yet another example of the codependent personality type I now know I was.

Nobody knew what was going on in my life. Nobody had any idea how sad, miserable and depressed I was feeling. Nobody knew how anxious and afraid I was. Nobody knew that I just wanted to be dead because of the choices I had made and the life I was living. All of this happened before I was pregnant with my first child. In the early days of the marriage, I could have just left the relationship and said that I'd made the biggest mistake of my life! I can say I didn't want to add to the devastation that I perceived my parents were in, but I was also scared to death of the word 'divorce'! What would Oma say? Or Jim's grandma? Thankfully, dysfunctional people learn to really live in the moment. If it was good, it was really good, simply because it wasn't bad!

There was no 'happily ever after' going on in our home as Jim and I would fight like cats and dogs – brutal arguments. Jim had friends who also fought in a similar way and those fights would ignite our arguments and fighting. This was our life and it never really changed over the next 17 years. The drug and alcohol abuse continued and became more habitual even though there were times we would agree that we had to clean up our act. Jim would go through periods of severe depression where he would just sit and drink and not speak. Initially, in his work environment a lot of drinking happened also. On Fridays after work, he and his co-workers would drink until late into the night and he wouldn't come home. Eventually, over the years, the drinking at work was almost every night. That was married life for me; I never knew where he was or if he was coming home.

Due to the deep loneliness I felt, and convinced I was missing out on all the fun, it became a simple decision to just go wherever Jim was so I would at least know where he was and what he was doing. Hiring a babysitter so I could go to the bar myself was worth it in Jim's eyes because then at least I wasn't bitching as much! I even ended up getting a job at the bar!

Hindsight being golden, I realized just a short time after my marriage ended that the void we often feel in our lives can be attributed to our 'love tanks' *not* being filled. While Jim would try to leave and be angry because his socks weren't washed (a sign that 'acts of service' was his preferred need or love language), I learned that 'spending time with people' is a primary love language of mine. *(*Recommended reading ***The Blessing*** by Smalley/Trent and ***The Five Love Languages*** by Gary Chapman.*)*

When Charlotte asked if I carried on this lifestyle during my pregnancies, I had to admit that during my first pregnancy I didn't even know I was pregnant. I remember going to a Pat Benatar concert and getting loaded out of my mind. Needless to say, I was absolutely horrified to learn a few weeks later that I was three months pregnant. All the way through the pregnancy I worried that my baby would be damaged due to that event. Quitting drinking each time, I also quit smoking as soon as I found out I was pregnant with Jasmine, but with Zach I just thought it wasn't that much of a deal. He was born a full pound and a half smaller and also an inch shorter than his sister, which I figure is proof that smoking during pregnancy does affect the birth weight and health of the baby. I did quit smoking again during my pregnancy with Caleb.

Jim and I ended up with three beautiful children in spite of our rocky road. We continued to fight outrageously, especially if we'd been drinking. Sadly, I could 'beat the crap' out of Jim just as much as he could do the same to me. My tendency was to hit, especially in response to Jim's mean, nasty, very sharp tongue. The verbal abuse would be so dishonoring and demeaning and was often harder to take than anything else. Begging him to shut up, "Stop! Please!" I would almost always turn around and smack Jim, and soon we would be 'beating the crap' out of each other again. Jasmine was merely months old when we had another major fist fight. I decided at that time that I was taking her and leaving. Jim wanted me gone, too, but was trying to remove Jasmine from my arms. After feeling as though Jasmine was literally being pulled limb from limb between us, I finally gave in. I said I wouldn't leave without her. He said that was fine and I was stuck with him until I was ready to leave without Jasmine because he'd never let me have her.

Now, as an advocate for battered women as well as women and children in high risk situations, I always remember that night. Because I was so afraid of losing my kids, especially to a father who seemed out of control, angry and unstable so much of the time, I felt I had no other choice than to stay. Jim's determination was always that he wanted me gone.

Since Jim and I had been married so young I was often asked to sing at the weddings of our friends. This became another point of contention in our marriage. If I dared to take a booking to sing, all hell would break loose. If it was a wedding of one of his friends, he would get so drunk and disorderly that it was a total embarrassment for me to sing with him acting out! Jim hated it when I sang and would try to persuade me not to sing. If I dared do it, he would belittle me unendingly. If I was scheduled to sing at a wedding and Jim was supposed to babysit, he would quite simply not show up to take responsibility for Jasmine so I could get ready and go. He tried to forbid me from doing so, making my life difficult every time! He said it was always my fault that he got drunk, that he was miserable. A couple of years into our marriage and he finally demanded I quit singing or else! Looking back, I know it was stupid that I bought into his ultimatum. I was just doing whatever I could not to rock the boat and to keep the peace; hopefully keeping him from drinking too and building some kind of a better life than what we'd been living!

I was faced with the horrifying belief that my family security was solely my responsibly. Obviously, that attitude is codependency with a capital "C", a word I never heard back then, but now understand. For so many reasons, I always had a codependent personality. In my childhood, I felt I had to keep the peace between my parents, walk on tiptoes to make sure my mom was happy, blah, blah, blah. Somehow, back then, I had felt it was my responsibility to keep our family life secure. It was an easy role to play.

I HATE MY LIFE! OH, GOD HELP ME! PLEASE, HELLO? ANYONE? J<><

Settling into this more serious version of life, I began getting really concerned about the lifestyle we were living. I knew it was time to shape up once and for all! My dad had been a 'pool playing, beer drinking' sort of guy. When I was three and my little sister just born, my parents gave their lives to Jesus and he cleaned up his act, which lead them to become a God-loving and church attending family. Somewhere in my thinking and belief system, I figured Jim and I would have a few years of rebellious living, drinking and partying, and then *we* would settle down like my dad had. I thought about it a lot and finally one night told Jim that I felt we had to quit drinking and clean up our act too. He looked at me as though I was from another planet! He asked what in the world was I talking about. Jim plainly told me that he had no intention of changing who he was and what he was doing because he loved his life! I asked how he could love falling down drunk and being hung over every second day, the fighting and carousing. Jim replied that I'd have to make a choice! It was his way or the highway.

He was not joking! It finally hit me that my validation, which was supposed to come from his loving me and being with me wasn't really there at all. Afraid to leave, it was at this time that I began crying out to God. Deep down, I felt that God had never left me. This really is the most powerful part of my story and has become a true encouragement for a lot of people since I started telling it.

I'd accepted the Lord as my Savior at six years of age. When I was being bullied and felt unloved during my childhood, or through the drinking and partying in my high school years, I always felt the presence of God on some level. Often when getting ready to go out drinking, I was aware we could die at any moment and I'd ask God to give me a few moments before I died to repent of the sin-sick life I was living! I knew the power of conviction of the Holy Spirit was on us to clean up our lives and it was a big deal for me. Stuck in this marriage situation, where I didn't feel loved at all, I needed to feel the love of God again. Some would say it was 'hope' I was missing and 'hope' I was seeking!

I started attending a Christian Women's group. It was a monthly gathering put on by Stonecroft Ministries. The fellowship and friendship of the ladies I met there became a huge support system to me. They had no idea what was going on in my life as I never, ever discussed it, but being part of that circle of friends helped me survive. I dedicate the song, *Circle of Friends,* to those I've met in moments like these!

> *We were made to love and be loved*
> *But the price this world demands will cost you far too much*
> *I spent too many lonely years just trying to fit in*
> *Now I've found a place in this circle of friends*
>
> *In a circle of friends we have one Father*
> *In a circle of friends we share this prayer*
> *That every orphaned soul will know and all will enter in*
> *To the shelter of this circle of friends*

Jasmine was just a wee baby when I joined the Christian Women's club and I felt blessed because Jim would babysit so I could get out. Over the next few years, this became my only real safe place. Jim wouldn't go to church and I believed the lie that I couldn't go to church unless I went with my husband. It is the lie of the enemy that if the whole family doesn't go to church, then the woman shouldn't go either. Although I don't know why I thought it, I believed it. Today, I encounter many women in my ministry who struggle with being the spiritual leader in their home. I find that a lot of women have the same perception I did and believe that lie, too!

The years with the Christian Women's group were very special to me and I eventually became part of their executive, which meant a twice-monthly meeting; one a prayer meeting and the other a regular group meeting. I would even sing occasionally at these events, although I never mentioned those times to Jim.

Two years apart, Zachariah James and Caleb James joined our family. My heart was full of love towards my beautiful, healthy and amazing children. Although I was desperately lonely in my marriage and fearful of the life we would have in the future as the drinking continued, I made the most of it. I often said to myself, I made my bed so now I had to lie in it! Snuggled close to my kidlins was a beautiful place to be so I survived and I would say I thrived as my girlfriends and I lived separate and apart in our happy housewife club!

I find it interesting that my now adult children really don't seem to have too many bad memories of the years we were together as a family. I personally credit this to my doing a very good job of hiding my fears and pain. I also found myself never belittling Jim, or making fun of him and worked hard not be angry. This would be part of the reason no one had a clue what was happening in my world! A lot of women and mothers in codependent situations will often belittle and begrudge their spouse. I was the opposite. I wanted to protect my children from the reality of who Jim could be. I would always try to make light of what went on because I didn't want my kids not to love him. This no doubt stemmed from the fact that the whole relationship started with my wanting him to be loved and that if only he could be loved, he would find a way to love himself, etc. etc. etc.

My discussions with Charlotte have enabled me to recognize the consequences of the old life. It has been an interesting part of my healing journey even over these last couple years. She's right; it has been hard at times. Only recently, I learned about the ways Jim lied and belittled me all through the early years and beyond. I do feel my kids have judged me more harshly than they ever judged their dad. I also long for the relationships I don't have, especially with my one son. However, I also realize it is my own fault as I struggled to portray a happy home and keep them from seeing the reality of my life with their dad. Like it or not, I would probably do it again if it meant saving them from the disillusionment I felt.

As life evolved and Jim's drug and alcohol abuse continued, he quit working as hard. He had been esteemed as one of the best automotive mechanics in southern Alberta. That began to change. Jim had the dream that if only he owned a farm, life would be better, that he'd finally be happy. He believed his birthright and his legacy had been stolen from him, another way he perceived that he had been wronged by life. We lived in Brooks then moved to Grassy Lake so he could work as a farmhand. Financial survival required that he return to automotive mechanics and a small business. Life as a hired hand *not* being his forte, our family moved back to the Brooks/Duchess area with the hope of farming for ourselves.

Jim tried to partner with his brother in Duchess for a season, but felt he had been horribly 'ripped off'. He and our son, Zach, had worked extremely hard, but were left without wages. We didn't even have grocery money. Times were so tough! It was just brutal and yet, as my mom and I were reminiscing recently about that time, we remembered an amazing story of God's provision for us in the midst of that storm. Action Parts, my parents' business, operated as a wholesaler of automotive parts. They were often offered sales incentives for the purchase of more shock absorbers, spark plugs, etc. During this time, when Jim and I literally had no grocery money, my parents received Safeway gift certificates based on their sales volume. Coming to visit every second Tuesday, they brought the gift certificates with them and while my dad called on customers for his business, mom and I would stock up on all the groceries and sundries needed!

Because of Jim's deep desire to farm, I made the decision to help him buy some equipment and get set up in a farming operation. I approached my parents who had built a successful family business over the past fifteen years. They were always concerned about us children and the legacy they would leave behind. Their estate planning and wills were discussed openly and the business was to be split three ways. I asked if they would be willing to give me the number of shares they intended for me to have so I could invest in a farm. My parents shared in that decision. In fact, I think we all truly felt that if Jim Barg could go farming and have animals of his own, then he could finally be happy. They met with their lawyers and I began cashing in my share of the family business. Over the next number of years, I watched my shares dwindle as my money bought equipment and cattle..

We bought our own operation in Purple Springs, Alberta. More of my early inheritance was invested in the cow/calf operation and the remodeling of our simple country home. I chose not to look back with regret. It was a matter of accepting that we do what we feel we must do.

Meanwhile though, everyone was holding his or her breath just hoping Jim would finally be happy.

Slam the door, Lord!
Please just Slam The DOOR!! J<><

I'm an idealistic person who always believes everything will turn out for the better. For Jim and me though, it was totally the opposite. The dream-come-true of having his own farm seemed to offer Jim no apparent joy. He started working less while drinking and using drugs more. Over the next couple of years, I got more heavily into drinking and drugs also. I could easily go through a bag of pot per week and forty ounces of scotch on a weekend. This continued until our marriage ended in April, 1994.

Jim had his own 'grow op' on the farm in the grain bins in Purple Springs and more and more drug paraphernalia around the house. He began to associate with a whole different group of people that literally scared me to death. We had three beautiful children in the second, fourth and sixth grades. I was very fearful and did not want 'those' people in my house or near my children. I knew Jim had a totally separate life going on out there, but I didn't care to be a part of it, not one single bit.

Due to this situation, I started drawing closer to God. Even though I was living a life full of alcohol and drug abuse, I was under the complete conviction of the Holy Spirit. Attending weekly church services, I asked if I could be baptized, sensing I needed to get out of the old life. On my way home from the bar or a party at night I would pray, "If I die on the way home tonight, please, could you just let me have things cleared up with you, Lord." I'd been praying this prayer since 1979, but quite frankly, I was becoming disgusted with my life... our lives! An intense need for eternal salvation and a deep desire to get out of the situation began to haunt me day in and day out.

I've since learned a lot about living in codependent relationships. It's not surprising that I worked really hard to prevent Christmas being destroyed for my kids. It was usually a nightmare. Early in our marriage Jim's parents hosted Christmas Eve. He would always come home from work drunk *that* evening. I hated the fact that we always arrived late to Christmas functions. The writing was obviously on the wall but I couldn't admit our life together would eventually be destroyed. In the early days, I feared every important date like Christmas and birthdays would be ruined. Now everyday was one of simple survival.

I knew our marriage was over on our final Christmas together when Jim left on Christmas Eve and did not come home for three days. I made the most of the holidays with the kids. Just as usual, we all pretended everything was okay. I had invited my parents to come for Christmas dinner later that week, even though it was very rare for me to cook a meal that big. Since my dad's favorite meal was turkey, I'd decided that would be a great Christmas gift for him. Jim had agreed with me to do this and yet he did not show up until much later than he should have. When he did, he was extremely drunk and disorderly. It was apparent that he was not even trying to pretend anymore.

Mental illness became prevalent in Jim's life. A demonic presence became evident in our home where one thing would be said and he or I would hear something entirely different. I would ask Jim what he wanted to eat and he would tell me eggs and bacon. I would go ahead and prepare the eggs and bacon and then he would come in and be so mad because that wasn't what he had asked for at all. Throwing something across the room, he'd say that he had asked for pork chops and applesauce! There was a spiritual oppression that came into our home the final couple of years, which was totally mind-boggling and frightening. Jim would tell people that I was losing my mind, yet I knew it was the other way around. Total chaos, fear and paranoia reigned!

Unwilling to give up on the marriage, I begged Jim to go for marriage counseling. We visited the office of a Christian marriage counselor. The appointment lasted about ten minutes. I shared my side of the story and Jim shared what he had to say and got up and walked out. He summarized his opinion by saying, "It's my way or the highway!" Then the marriage counselor looked at me and said, "Look at me. Look straight into my eyes. You realize your marriage is over?"

I said, "No!"

"I am telling you that your marriage is over," the counselor repeated.

I left there feeling totally devastated and wondering what kind of help that was supposed to be. After all, what kind of idiotic Christian counselor can tell us that our marriage is over? How can that even be an option, I wondered?

We had a friend who was diagnosed with bipolar disorder who everyone was saying had snapped and was found sitting in a corner crying. I began to wonder if that was what was happening with Jim or if that was what would happen to him. Again, my only solace became crying out to God and asking for His protection over the kids and me. I began to fear for my life and was worried that Jim was plotting to kill me. In fact, he once asked me to go out to check the cows with him and I was convinced that he was going to shoot me. I don't know to this day whether that was a drug-induced paranoid delusion or total Holy Spirit protection. I used the cell phone and stayed on the phone with the kids the entire way home because I was so afraid of being shot. I remember an urgency to get back home to the house. Jim absolutely hated me and all I did and was involved in. His contempt was not hidden at all.

In the spring of 1994, I served on many municipal committees, local hall boards and regional task forces. I participated on thirteen different councils and committees. I had a full-time job in Lethbridge (one and a half hours away) where I worked in television advertising. I was also the stations representative for the community of Taber. The chaos in our home was unbelievable from one day to the next. One example was his threat to kill me if I didn't quit my job. He wanted me home making dinner and doing laundry. Jim was so desperate in his desire for me to stay at home that he threatened to take the car away from me. Consequently, I prepared a letter of resignation. When I was about to leave for work that day, I told him the letter was written and I would give it to my boss! Again, Jim went ballistic and said, "Don't you dare quit your f----- job! You can't quit! That's the only way we have food on the table!"

There was no money coming in from the farm and, as usual, Jim blamed it on someone 'screwing him' in a deal or betraying him. Always it was somebody else's fault. My job provided the only income we had at that time. In anger, Jim told me to get an apartment and stay in town in order to work more hours. Things were constantly changing from day to day. I didn't know what to do. Total confusion reigned again.

Leaving for work early that morning, with a plan to resign from my job and with Jim's words resonating in my ears telling me not to, I finally threw my hands up in the air! In tears, I drove into the city and told God that he would simply have to 'slam the door' on whatever was wrong. If I was supposed to quit my job, then He should have me fired or laid off. I wanted some kind of sign that I shouldn't be working there. If I was supposed to cancel my obligation to the municipal planning committee, or cease to be part of the rural tourism project and the town hall committee, fine! Whatever God wanted, I pled with Him to show me the way and to 'slam the door'.

I continued to work that day and nothing happened; in fact, they loved me there. My thoughts then turned to the possibility of getting an apartment in the city so I could work more hours.

When Charlotte asked if anyone knew what was going on all this time, I said, "Definitely not!" Alcoholic homes are great at keeping secrets. In later years, I learned that Jim had been telling horrible stories about me all over town. He even had our middle child convinced that the two of them would run away together and escape being with me any longer.

Did the alcoholism affect the children? Even though there was no direct discussion about the subject, our children were not stupid. They all knew that mom and dad were unhappy and they took on different roles within the alcoholic home. Our youngest son, Caleb, was the joker; the happy-go-lucky guy always telling jokes. Our daughter, Jasmine, the eldest, was the caretaker; she looked after the house and made sure everything always looked nice. She adopted the mothering role and always made sure the boys were safe and okay and prevented any 'rocking of the boat'. Zach, our middle son, would get up at four o'clock in the morning to go check the cattle and calves, taking on responsibility beyond his years. He did the driving for Jim and took him from yard to yard and intended to be a partner with his dad. Years of counseling and dealing with the reality of my life have helped me to understand this. Certainly I could not recognize it at the time.

As I drove home after the day at work and nothing had happened, I asked God what else there could be that needed to shift. Again I asked

Him to please "slam the door" on whatever it was because I was exhausted and just didn't know what to do anymore.

I got home and approached the door only to find it locked. This was confusing since I could see the kids inside the house. The kids said, "Mommy go away. Just go."

I said, "Open the door. Just open the door and let me in."

Jim came to the door and told me that I wasn't welcome there and had to leave. I told him there was no way I was going anywhere without my kids. I agreed to go if that was what he wanted, but I would never leave without them!

The screaming continued back and forth through the door. Jim's foul mouth just added to the intensity of the arguing. He went and grabbed a rifle and brought it to the door. Now the kids started screaming and telling him that he couldn't do this kind of thing. I was going to call the police. As I turned to leave, Jim opened the door to follow me. Ever so quickly I turned and rushed into the house to make sure the kids were okay. I discovered that Jim had loaded 32 different guns around the perimeter of our little country kitchen. On the table, I saw a huge pile of ammunition. He cocked his rifle and said, "I'm going to kill you! I'm done with you! I hate you! I want you out of here! You have to go!"

"I am not going anywhere without these kids," I stated emphatically. It is interesting to note that I wasn't afraid of him at all, but simply thought he was some kind of idiot to think a mother would leave without her kids.

All hell broke loose! Words cannot fully describe the chaos that ensued. There was pushing and shoving. The kids, crying hysterically, were sent to their rooms being told we would work things out. All of a sudden, Jim grabbed me and was dragging me out the door. He threw me off the step and 'slammed the door'.

Lying in the dirt, I heard the door slam and thought, "Oh surely, God, You're not slamming the door on my marriage?"

I got up and started to bang on the door. Now I was beyond angry. The cuss words started flowing from my mouth just as easily as from Jim's. One of the kids came and opened the door for me. When I got to the entranceway, Jim barred the doorway and again told me that he was going to kill me. He picked me up and threw me out the door again. This time I was injured and had the wind knocked out of me. Once again, 'the door slammed'. In my mind I knew God was 'slamming the door' on my marriage and a quiet peace came over me.

I thought about many things as I lay there on the ground. I hoped that my Oma would forgive me for being done with my marriage because I just couldn't do it anymore. I also hoped my mom and dad could forgive me. I thought about my kids and prayed that God would protect them. I prayed for wisdom to deal with the mess I'd made of my life. All I knew as I lay in the dirt was that we'd never be able to survive financially. We were already on the brink of foreclosure because Jim wasn't making any money. Our expenses far exceeded our income every month. I realized I had stayed because I'd invested so much of my legacy and would probably lose it all, but I also knew I was done! I was afraid the banker and my parents would discover our situation very quickly. I was so scared and had no idea how we would ever survive.

I got up and brushed myself off, walked through the unlocked door and told Jim that I would leave, but I had to take the kids with me just for now. Leaving Jim to settle down seemed like the thing to do at the moment. He looked like a raving lunatic and had been doing crazy things for weeks. His behavior was not only a concern to me, but had also become a concern to other people in the community. "Just let us go," I asked him, "please."

As he stood there with his rifle pointed at me, he cocked it again and told me that he should just kill me. The bedroom door opened and Zach, who was only eleven, came out cocking a .22 pointed at his dad and said, "If you kill Mom, then I'll have to kill you, Dad." It was a moment of illumination. Everything stopped. Jim put his gun down then and told us to go.

He picked up the phone and dialed a number. I heard him say, "Heidi! This is Jim. Jodi and the kids are leaving right now and if they don't get to you within the hour, it's because I've killed them all. They are on their way to you and we will discuss things at a later date. Just wanted you to know they are on the way." The remarkable thing about this was that there was no way that I would have been going to my parents' place in Medicine Hat. I didn't want them to know what was happening in my life and especially that it had come to this! Plus, my job was in Lethbridge in the totally opposite direction. All the people that I hung out with and that I called friends lived for the most part between Purple Springs and

Lethbridge. Since Jim had made that call, though, I knew I had to go to Medicine Hat.

As we were running to leave, Jim told us that if we even looked out the back window, he would kill us all. We sped off and got as far as the Burdett Bar. I stopped to get a six-pack of beer to go with the bag of pot in my pocket and then I called the police. I was afraid Jim would end up killing somebody because he was so out of control. I spoke to a 911-dispatch center and told them I was heading to my parents' home in Medicine Hat. The city police were there and waiting for us before we arrived. That was how my parents found out we were coming to their house.

If you think there's a contradiction in the last statement, you are absolutely right. For years I told my story exactly like this until one night when my mom heard me sharing my testimony in a concert setting and questioned me about it. She said there had never been a phone call to them that night. Jim did not call my parents at all. He faked it! Interestingly, he had manipulated things, wanting me to think that my parents were waiting for us at the other end. It wasn't until we walked in the door that my parents knew what had happened. The police watched over us all for the next number of weeks as Jim's threats against me were taken very seriously.

As a keynote speaker today, I am able to share our family's story. It is very true that long term drug and alcohol abuse leads to mental illness. Anyone like Jim, who had so much potential for his life and so many gifts and talents, can be destroyed by mental illness. These are the consequences of long time drug and alcohol abuse. Getting clean can make so much of a difference. My children witnessed the difference between a parent that chose to get clean and a parent that chose not to.

When I share my story, I always tell how we had to flee for our lives and ended up 'homeless'. Hopelessness and homelessness in this instance included the psychological place we found ourselves in. We lost absolutely all sense of security and literally awoke one morning with no roof to call our own. Setting aside my pride, admitting my need and asking for help, was the first step to rebuilding my life. So many people are so alone in their circumstances, but my parents allowed us to step into their home and provided a place of sanctuary. My brother and sister and their spouses also embraced us all with intense love and comfort. They helped me to rebuild my life so that the children and I weren't forced to live under a bridge or on the street. I dedicate my rendition of the Paul Overstreet song, **Love Can Build A Bridge,** to them.

I'd gladly walk across the desert
With no shoes upon my feet
To share with you the last bite
Of bread I had to eat
I would swim out to save you
In your sea of broken dreams
When all your hopes are sinking
Let me show you what love means

Love can build a bridge
Between your heart and mine
Love can build a bridge
Don't you think it's time?

Peace in the midst of the storm. J<><

During our drive to Medicine Hat that fateful night, I prayed and prayed. I asked God to forgive me! I asked the kids to forgive me for the horrible mess our lives had become! I remembered the prayer I prayed when I was a child. I'd never taught the original version to my kids, changing the words to "angels watch me through the night and wake me with the morning light"! I'd never liked thinking about dying every night as I went to sleep as a child so wanted to save my kids from that, but on this night I prayed the original version of the prayer with all of my kids.

Now I lay me down to sleep,
I pray the Lord my soul to keep.
If I should die before I wake,
I pray the Lord my soul to take.

Our lives were in jeopardy and it was completely possible we wouldn't survive. Jim was really that out of control. Police protection was arranged and everyone began living in absolute prayer! With me and the kids living in my parents' basement, I often testify to how their unconditional love and welcome helped me to rebuild my life. Since they never had any idea of what we had lived through, it was totally mind-boggling for them to hear stories of what had gone on.

As I was lying on the floor that first night, I pondered what my life had become. I was working at a television station and had a different group of friends. My husband didn't even know what I did at my job and probably couldn't have cared less. We'd actually lived totally separate lives. Now here I was, starting over!

My immediate boss was gay and although I loved my life among my coworkers, I'd been feeling her interest in me! Realizing it might be a really bad idea to end up there, I concluded there was no way I could go to Lethbridge without a nickel to my name. I couldn't even afford groceries, so having a mortgage or rent payment was out of the question. As the anxiety and fear grew, I began crying out to God and told Him how I couldn't believe that I had made such a mess. I told Him I was so sorry!

Weeping while I was lying on the floor that night, it struck me how God's love for me had never really changed. From becoming a Christian as a little girl at six years old and all through the years, I realized that God's love really was important to me. Having a Christian home was something Jim and I had fought about a lot. I knew I wasn't willing to live my life without God. I also knew there would be no more excuses because this was all on my shoulders now.

My prayer to God was, "Thank you for saving us. Thank you for keeping us alive tonight as we were driving." However, I became filled with anxiety. How am I going to survive and make this work? I poured my heart out to God.

In that exact moment, I heard the audible voice of God for the first and only time in my life. "Be still!" I heard. Two simple words in the midst of my tears, cares and concerns. Hearing those words I knew that God was with me no matter what. The same peace I'd felt earlier, when I knew God was slamming the door on my marriage, was once again impressed upon me. I knew that God wouldn't desert me. He was right there with me! "Be still!" The same peace experienced at that moment is with me today. God powerfully gave me the deep assurance that He was with me and although I had no clue what tomorrow might bring, I knew He was with me and everything was going to be okay. *I Know Who Holds Tomorrow,* is a great song that speaks to exactly this kind of moment in our lives!

I don't know about tomorrow,
I just live from day to day.
I don't borrow from its sunshine,
For its skies may turn to gray.
I don't worry o'er the future,
For I know what Jesus said,

And today I'll walk beside Him,
For He knows what is ahead.
Many things about tomorrow,
I don't seem to understand;
But I know Who holds tomorrow,
And I know Who holds my hand.

It actually isn't all about me!
Get over yourself and help 'reach the world!' J<><

One of the significant things that happened in those first few nights occurred when I was lying in bed, pondering life and asking God to help me survive. There are always times of desperation when one wonders why one is still here. I sensed that God had a reason and purpose for my life. The perseverance of my Oma when she first came to Canada kept coming back to me. Oma had never given up and had believed that God had a purpose for her life. I needed to believe that just to be able to keep living and moving.

I sensed very strongly that I needed to go back to church. Unfortunately, my only thought was that they were all hypocrites there and I hated them. Jim and I had built a life on hatred of the church. We both believed that church people were two-faced pretenders. We had felt that if only those people had loved us, then our lives might have been different.

In the dark of the night, (and I will *always* remember that night), God spoke to my spirit with the undeniable truth that I was just as much a hypocrite as every hypocrite I had ever judged! I had totally 'missed the boat'. Just like people have the sense of their life passing right before their eyes in death, my life flashed before my eyes. God's plan for my life had been to reach out to people. God began to remind me of the faces and names of people that He had meant for me to reach out to in the foyer of the churches I'd attended through the years. I had spent years waiting for others to reach out to me, but now God was showing me people from the past twenty seven years that He had wanted me to show His love to. Since I had been so consumed by the fact that nobody had been reaching out to me, I had been of no earthly good. This rocked my world! To be considered by God a worse hypocrite than any hypocrite I had ever judged was a fate worse than death!

Weeping and filled with remorse, all I could do was seek God's forgiveness. And God, being so merciful, graciously forgave me. However, for the next year He constantly reminded me every time I walked into a church, "You are the solution."

My new mantra became "I am His hands and His feet. I am the one He has put here for such a time as this to reach out to these people."

That first Sunday when I made the decision to go back to church, I made myself available to God and asked Him to show me just one person that needed to know that He loved them. I wanted to boldly be God's hands and feet and to be His love in this hurting world. I wished to make amends for not being that person in the past.

> [3] May the God and Father of our Lord Jesus Christ be blessed! He is the compassionate Father and God of all comfort. [4] He's the one who comforts us in all our trouble so that we can comfort other people who are in every kind of trouble. We offer the same comfort that we ourselves received from God.

> 2 Cor.1:3-5

My parents had taken the kids to get them settled in Sunday school and I sat alone in my car. They had actually wanted me to take the day off to be alone and rest. I knew I needed to go back to church, but I was afraid and embarrassed. It is hard when you have judged so harshly and the Lord shows you so clearly that you have been wrong, and that you were a huge part of the problem regarding all the hypocritical, unloving Christians in the world!

I got out of the car and headed toward the church, but with very little self-confidence. Again I asked God to show me somebody who needed His love and He surely did. I arrived at the door at the exact moment that another young lady got there. We introduced ourselves to one another. When I asked her if this was her church, she said she had never been there before. I said, "Well, this isn't my church either, but would you like to sit with me?"

Not only did she sit with me that day, but a good friendship grew between us. We shared many conversations from that day onward. We immersed ourselves in a 'Christian singles' lifestyle and became part of a lovely group of individuals who were committed to Christ and lived morally upright lives. As a group, we enjoyed evenings out weekly and even a bus tour to the Passion Play in Drumheller that summer. As the fall ministry kick-off began in our church, my friend asked me if I'd go to choir with her.

That particular church had an awesome choir that had really been ministering to me since I'd arrived there that spring. However, I tried to tell the girl that I wasn't that good at singing even though I'd sung a long time ago. Then I sensed God telling me that I needed to go to choir to be a support to her.

The best part of going to choir turned out to be the fellowship and coffee we shared afterward. Usually there was a whole group of us that went out for coffee, but one particular night it was just the two of us.

My girlfriend said, "It is rather odd that it should just be the two of us, but I somehow feel that I am supposed to tell you my story. I feel like I have to tell you something."

I said, "Sure. Go ahead."

The girl got serious and told me to really listen to what she had to say. "Do you remember that first day that you met me at church?"

I told her I did remember because that was a special day for me as well. It was the day that I had changed my whole philosophy and had decided I was going to reach out to some stranger.

What I heard next were these words: "What you don't know about that day that I came to church, was that I came for one reason and one reason only. The only reason I came to church that day was to make peace with God. I had planned my suicide for that afternoon. The only reason I am alive today is because you asked me if I would sit with you."

The amazing part of this story is that God had never revealed to me my girlfriends hidden brokenness. I had no idea whatsoever that my friend was also a 'hurting sparrow' and that He needed me to reach out to her. God knew that He had to use somebody to save her. I liken it to being two 'broken sparrows' God brought together to help each other heal.

My friend was a child youth worker and had all sorts of helpful information for me on how help my children. All this time I thought I'd been the one receiving so much from her. Now I found out that God had also been using me.

She also told me that if she had died that day, she would not have had an eternity with Jesus. It was only during the summer, at the Passion Play, that she had accepted the Lord.

Through the next few years, I would wake up every morning and ask God to show me just one more person who needed to know His love. I would feel the prompting of the Holy Spirit to approach someone and would say, "I feel like God just really wants you to know He loves you today!" I laugh out loud about some of the crazy reactions some people had to these kinds of moments, but I remember a few of those stories as being so-o-o-o awesome!

I had watched Oprah one afternoon. I'd had a very unsettled feeling about the book which was being reviewed and had actually turned off the show. The next day, while shopping at Superstore, I was in the card aisle when I noticed a young woman on the opposite side of the aisle looking at that same book. I remember thinking, "She just needs to know You love her, Lord." I suddenly felt the Lord telling me to go tell the young lady that He loved her. I looked up and down the aisle seeing another woman just down from us. I remember saying to God, "Why don't You ask *that* lady to go tell her that You love her?" But no, I knew it was a message for me! I approached the young woman and simply said, "Hi! Excuse me, but I think God just wants you to know He loves you today!" With that, the woman put the book back on the shelf and with eyes full of tears turned to me. She said, "I said to God this very morning, if You even exist You had better show yourself to me because I'm done with You!" Through my wide eyed smile, I said, "Wow!" Turning away I said, "Well, okay then, good-bye." Today, I laugh about how I just walked away because I did not have a clue what to do next. But I also know that in spite of *me*, that young woman definitely had an encounter with the living God that day, eh? I hope people agree! It was an awesome moment! LOL!

Another time that I recall from that season is when I was at a gas station. I felt the Lord telling me to give five dollars to a young woman across the parking lot. I remember thinking at the time that five bucks wasn't much at all, but I was willing to do it. As I approached the young woman I said, "I felt God telling me to give you five dollars." The young woman smiled hugely and said as her eyes filled with tears, "I came here even though I had no money for milk for my baby and now I'll be able to buy milk *and* a loaf of bread!" For me, the most remarkable part of this story has always been that God did all that through me, even though I was like a broken clay pot myself. His love flowed through me to change lives!

A new life begins! J<><

In the days and weeks that followed our move into my parents' home, things were interesting to say the least! There were police reports that Jim was going totally crazy out in our home area. I had the kids at home with me during those early days of commotion and unrest. It was stressful because they wanted to go to the mall and to go out. I wanted them to be able to go to school and yet felt I needed to protect them. I believed a small urban school would be safer than a large city school.

My parents came alongside me at this time and were able to assure me that there was still money coming to me from the family business, and they wanted to help me build a house and start over. A new subdivision was going up in the little town of Dunmore and it seemed like the perfect place for me to start rebuilding our lives. Dunmore also provided access to the rural school environment I wanted for the kids. They were enrolled and started attending school and life seemed to settle down a little more.

However, it wasn't long before I started getting calls from the school. Jim had been spotted in the area. The police were aware of his presence and were often on high alert. I give great credit to the principal of the school, Brian Angelic, and his staff as he so aptly and efficiently handled the safety situation for the kids. The whole school community were committed to keeping my kids safe. They never once gave the impression that they didn't want the kids there because of the conflict. Rather, they assured me beyond a shadow of a doubt that my kids would be kept completely safe there. They were preparing for lockdowns in the school before the term 'lockdown' was ever heard.

Once things settled down from the initial chaos of leaving Jim, and I got adjusted to life as a single mom, things started going pretty well.

'Plugging into' the community of faith, I learned that I was precious and wonderfully made. I often felt God wrapping His arms of love around me. I also took drug and addictions counseling. I was blown away as I said I needed my "higher power" to be Father, Son and Holy Spirit and discovered my assigned counselor was also a Christian. It was during my time in his office at the Alberta Alcohol & Drug Abuse Commission (AADAC) that I began to understand that I had been married to an alcoholic, and that we had been living a life of codependency that was literally 'text book'. My eyes were opened to so much truth I'd never known. I was stunned to learn that the way we lived – the way almost everyone we knew lived – was not necessarily the way life had to be! I remember telling my counselor I just wanted to live a 'normal' life. A very profound statement I heard back then was "There is no such thing as 'normal'!" From my counselor I learned that success comes from simply learning to live with, cope and overcome whatever level of dysfunction we're faced with.

The most difficult thing for me to hear was that my children would likely end up marrying substance abusers or being substance abusers themselves. That is not the type of thing any mother wants to hear. With the AADAC involvement in my life, and with very good training and advice, I learned what types of signs to watch for in my kids.

Over the weeks and months that followed my decision to attend church regularly, I was surprised to learn that everyone in the church seemed to know about me and my story. I had no idea how everyone knew of my situation, but every Sunday it seemed another little old white-haired lady would walk up to me and tell me that she was praying for me and my kids. Eventually, I found out that my mom and dad had been the ones who told everyone about us and our situation. I came to accept that random people were praying for us. One Sunday, everything changed as another lady asked, "Jodi, *how* can we pray for you? *How* do we pray for you and your children?" I was caught a bit off guard. Nobody had asked me that before. This moment became a significant step in my healing journey.

I've since realized there had been 'word curses' on my life for many years. My attitude toward prayer was one of them and had been with me since I was a young girl. I had been playing at my friend's place when the girl's dad came in for lunch. They lived on a farm and this was back in the day of party lines (where several people's phones were on one line and you could hear the conversations of the others when you picked up the receiver). Over lunch, the girl's parents discussed some calls that he wanted his wife to make for him and that was all good. However, when he got up to leave and was checking to be sure she would make those calls, he said, "And be careful what you say on that phone today. These party lines are as bad as the prayer chain at church."

When this little white-haired lady spoke to me that day, I realized that I had always protected myself from the prayer chain! I had had a cynical distrust of what it meant to have people discussing or sharing my needs. I also realized I was in a season where God was breaking down all the barriers and dispelling the lies that I had accumulated over my life. It wasn't rocket science to me that day. I realized that I had a choice to make, a choice to allow myself to be transparent as a part of the church community and to accept the love of God being extended toward me. As that lady stood there with so much patience and so much grace, I began to weep and said, "I'm having a horribly difficult time." Explaining some of what was happening I said I didn't know how to help my hurting son who was feeling so abandoned and angry. I shared how overwhelmed I felt at times not knowing how to help my children through our difficulties. The lady ever so gently put her hand over my hand and said, "You are not alone."

Once more I realized that the way God loves us in this world is through His people. For years I'd missed out on the fellowship of the body of Christ because of the lies I had believed and the hypocrisy I focused upon. I think that isolation is one of the greatest strategies Satan uses in our world. As long as we are not part of fellowship, we will not feel the fullness of God's love for us.

It was a very powerful time for me as I got involved in women's ministries! I was able to learn from the wisdom of so many as I learned to verbalize my cares and concerns. I 'plugged into' the fellowship to be found. I grew in my understanding of the Bible and the ways of the Lord. It seemed like every time I turned around there was a Bible study starting up that dealt with exactly what I needed to hear and exactly what I needed to learn.

Accepting the love extended... J<><

Upon beginning my 'new life' in 1994, clean and sober, I know that having close friends and relationships in my new church family was instrumental in getting through the most difficult years. I immersed myself in the church in order to survive my circumstances and to do so victoriously. During this season, I was part of a church family whose ministry slogan was "TO LOVE, MEND, TRAIN AND SEND". The first time I walked into Hillcrest Church in Medicine Hat, those words were written right on the church wall. There was a deliberate, intentional belief among that body of believers that we had to *intentionally* love others. Whether it was from the older folk who went to prayer breakfasts with my parents or from the ladies I met through women's ministries, I experienced love. Through the great ministry programs and 'small group' philosophy my church embraced, there was always something offered to help me be mended, healed, restored and trained.

My friend (a specialist in child and youth work) gave me a wealth of information and wisdom. She was there for me during the stresses with the kids as they faced some of the brutal realities around them, and as we dealt with our hurts and hang- ups. Things were pretty tough for the kids at times.

As I said, I came to realize during those early days that the desire of Satan is to keep us isolated. I began to see how the enemy worked in my insecurities and judgments. It is so easy for us to sit back and wait for others to love and reach out to us. If Satan can make us feel lonelier when we are at church than when we are actually alone, then he has done his job well. For twenty years, I experienced this before gaining the victory and becoming a useful vessel for the Lord.

Our focus has to be on how we can be useful as a part of the church by showing love and kindness to others in and out of the church building. No longer the hypocrite, I learned that I could be the one to walk across the room and ask about going out for coffee and taking time for others. Volunteer involvement became important to me. Our lives should focus on reaching out and serving others.

One of the decisions I made during this time was to become a member of the church. They were offering 'new member' classes and I knew I needed to step into the community with both feet, something I had never done before in my thirty-year faith journey. The lead pastor at the church was a valuable teacher and mentor. Pastor Dan Reinhart took me and others through the 'Spiritual Gifts' class and we were all tested. I discovered my compassion gifts to be super high as well as the fact that I was an 'exhorter'. This explained why I'd always struggled so much with seeing the hypocrisy among believers and wanting to change the world! LOL!

Being in a community of faith and rebuilding my life, I completely believed I would never be able to get remarried. Growing up Mennonite, I thought there was a Biblical scripture that said I could never remarry. Deep down I also felt a heavy spirit of condemnation for my failed marriage. One of the significant changes that happened by being part of these women's ministry groups was that ladies started coming alongside me to show me differently. I began to understand that there is nothing we can do to make ourselves approved by God. There is nothing we can do to save ourselves from ourselves. God's grace and mercy came in the form of Jesus and *nothing* can keep us from His grace and mercy. He will work through whatever the circumstances are in our lives. I began to understand that I am precious in His sight. More importantly, I was also discovering that as long as I have breath, God is not finished with me. God has a plan for my life!

I had a mentor whose husband of many, many years finally came out of the closet and left her for a gay man. She was divorced and was struggling with what she was supposed to do. Her life was destroyed. We both believed we'd have to be single forever. God began breaking down that lie in her life. She took it upon herself to share a book about marriage after divorce with me and other women like us. It seemed every page broke down the lies I had believed. My friend's sharing was proof of something I had begun to sense... that 'our misery can become our ministry' if we let it.

There are people that need to know there is life after divorce. I was one of them. Another lady who had remarried many years earlier shared her story with me. At the time though, I wondered why God was telling me all of this. I was okay with never being married again. In God's divine plan, I see now, He knew that He had to break down the lies that had been instilled in me. Through Bible studies and the testimonies of some of these ladies, I was finally able to tell God that whatever His plan was for my life, I would accept it. I would never go looking for someone to marry, but if that was His will then I would trust Him to work it out. Today as Bob and I travel, I've thought of creating a journal of all the many stories of 'hope found after divorce' that we have since heard.

Pride is often a struggle for single moms on our own trying to make ends meet. I had no choice but to put that pride aside and accept a job that was offered to me. If I had another word of advice to those striving to make it on their own, I'd say, "It really does take a community to save a life!" Accepting the love and opportunities extended to me was how my new life could begin.

I was able to get a job in the family business. My brother Jason was actually the one who came along and offered me a job. This was rather difficult for me since I had already sold my birthright by taking out my shares in the family business years earlier. The job offered was well suited to my gifts and talents! There was a whole aspect to our automotive parts business that nobody had ever had the time to delve into. Jason said they felt that since I had experience in the promotions and advertising department of the TV station, I could be a tremendous asset. They had advertisements that needed to be written, promotions and all kinds of customer loyalty programs that needed to be handled. Jason told me there was nobody on staff to handle those things. Initially, I felt that they were just trying to create a job for me. He and my brother-in-law, Kerry, were beginning to take over the business from mom and dad and they soon convinced me that I truly *was* needed in that position. In fact, I was really an answer to prayer!

There were times in my new job that I definitely saw God show up and prove His faithfulness as well. This occurred through new relationships with manufacturers' representatives. So many of these fellows (who sold tools and parts to us) told stories of how they and their children had also gone through horrible circumstances similar to mine and survived. As they shared, I'd find myself just bawling sometimes. It was awesome how I was able to find encouragement for my situation from them and their stories, care and compassion.

One of the great examples of how God took care of me after my marriage ended occurred when I was driving down the road one day. The police pulled me over and were going to take my car. Everything Jim and I had owned was being seized. Jim was in jail now and the minute he was incarcerated, the bank foreclosed on us. The only way the bank could recover some of their investment was by selling off our farm assets. Everything was going to auction including the children's toys in the yard. Right out from under me that day, the Sheriff took my car! Walking home, I cried out to God in total desperation and frustration. My parents owned a second vehicle and told me that I could just use it. Then my dad came home one day on his way to a golf tournament. He's an avid golfer. He told me, "You know what? I'm going to win a car for you today."

I replied, "Yeah, right. And how do you think you are going to do that?"

"Well, there are a lot of prizes attached to these kinds of tourneys. One of the prizes is a used car for closest to the pin."

About eight hours later, he called me and said, "Guess what? I got you a car!" I burst into tears. Once again, God showed me how much He cared about us. My dad's team had won the car and they all knew about my situation. These men agreed the car should go to me! That car was my transportation for quite some time afterward. LOL!

RETHINKING... BE NOT CONFORMED TO THE WAY
THE WORLD DOES THINGS BUT RENEW
YOUR MIND. HMMM... J<><

When I hear people say that God doesn't care about the little and insignificant details of our lives, I'm quick to tell them differently. I *know* He loved and cared about me enough to put me in a church that had a concrete plan to help people just like me in my time of need. As far as I'm concerned, that was no coincidence! Because of the intentional mandate the church had, the love that I sensed and felt from those people was incredible. I realized how different my early years of Christian Women's Club and church attendance would have been if only I had reached out even once to those people and asked them to pray for me. I began to rethink the attitude I'd always had of keeping things 'private'.

The women's ministry in my church was a safe place where I was welcomed, befriended and encouraged. People shared their stories with one another. I was asked in the early days of my transformation if I would share my story at one of their meetings. It wasn't something I was comfortable doing, but God knew it was something I was supposed to do. I felt as though I was being catapulted into being open, honest and transparent about my life! I remember how, even that first time, people were moved and inspired by what I shared. They encouraged me and told me that lives would be changed through the sharing of my story. Even though I didn't feel qualified to walk through those doors, I did it in the power of the Spirit. It was wonderful to allow myself to be loved by the community of faith and to grow in my understanding of who God was.

After some time, I was asked to lead a Bible study. There had to be some kind of material selected and subject matter determined. One day I asked God what His plan was for this new ladies' Bible study. Suddenly I remembered an opportunity I'd had to get some Bibles. In the back of the Bible, there were some simple questions about who God was and such; helps for a new believer. God reminded me of that New Believer's Bible and I dug it out. It had little write-ups about how precious we are, what amazing creatures we are and how much He loves us. Of course, I'd probably heard this stuff before, but I didn't *know* it in my heart. The lies I had believed filled my mind. God's Word says, **"Be renewed by the transforming of your mind." (Romans 12:2b)** The study would address how amazing we are and that God's mercy is so great toward us because He loves us so much. All of this led me to rethink who I was and some of the things I had always believed about myself. A major healing journey started that day as I looked at another verse for the first time in my life. Zephaniah 3:17 states that the God of the universe sings for joy because of me! That He loves me unconditionally, I am amazing in His sight, He knows me, is with me and is willing to battle for me. I was rocked as these truths filled my mind and joy filled my heart!

I began to feel that the reason Satan had so deliberately destroyed my life was because he knew I was created to be dangerous to him as a champion for the Kingdom of God! I believe when you start understanding your identity in Christ, Satan begins to get really scared. His number one tool against us is deception, when we misunderstand how beautifully and wonderfully we are made. God started bringing into my life others who had also been on this 'hurt and healing' type of journey. I was very encouraged by the stories they told of how God had been faithful to them when they had been going through struggles and trials.

My first husband came back after his year in jail and asked for the opportunity to start over. We tried to make it work, but things were back to being irreconcilable very quickly. He promised he would honor the "no drinking, no drugs" philosophy I had incorporated in my new home, but he was soon drinking again. He began to live a life separate and apart from me, one I wasn't invited to participate in.

During an attempted family holiday to Hawaii to visit my in-laws, I was distressed and discouraged by Jim's sullen and disengaged behavior. It was paradise and such a beautiful place to be and yet he was completely detached. It wasn't until we returned home that Jim explained that he had wanted to 'literally drive off a cliff' and had tried to do so while out with the rental car that week. I realized he was still dealing with depression or other mental illness, and like it or not, I couldn't *fix* the situation at all. 'Let Go and Let God' became a way of life as I gave Jim back to God every day – knowing his life, his choices and his addictions were not my responsibility.

My energy was directed toward prayer for my kids and becoming a real advocate for other women in difficult marriages, or those who felt very lonely and discouraged. The more I connected with God through Jesus Christ, the more I was able to deal with what seemed like a desperate and doomed situation! Overcoming my hopelessness and depression *was* possible in Jesus' name! I lived, walked and overcame as I ministered to others who also felt stuck in difficult situations and needed to find strength outside their own efforts. One of the key phrases Bob and I use in our ministry today is YOUR MISERY WILL BECOME YOUR MINISTRY. Looking back on the ministry opportunities I have had since that time, I'd say this is truer than most of us are willing to believe!

My involvement in the music ministry at church was a huge blessing to me also. God grew my love for Him through the music I felt so honored to share during worship services and through the choir. Pastor Randy Feere was a wonderful and gentle leader. Through the years, small groups became a part of each choir practice. Each of the members shared their life experiences, fellowship, prayer requests and praise items at some point in the evening. I prioritized this time and the Lord ministered to me through the beautiful body of Christ. I dedicate the song, ***How Beautiful,*** to every one of those friends. My attitude of gratitude grew because of the fellowship I found in the family of God.

How beautiful the radiant bride
Who waits for her Groom with His light in her eyes
How beautiful when humble hearts give
The fruit of pure lives so that others may live
How beautiful, how beautiful,
How beautiful is the body of Christ

How beautiful the feet that bring
The sound of good news and the love of the King
How beautiful the hands that serve
The wine and the bread and the sons of the Earth
How beautiful, how beautiful,
How beautiful is the body of Christ

One of the great initiatives at my church was to invite as many as possible in the worship arts department to attend 'Breakforth'. An intensive worship arts convention hosted in Edmonton, Alberta it was attended by as many as three to six thousand people every January. I learned so much about myself at these conventions including how to help people *engage* in their worship experience. Traveling those Alberta winter roads with friends led to hours of conversation and sharing. Every class taken added to the wisdom and discipleship, healing and celebration I was learning to walk in.

My leadership role continued to grow at Hillcrest as the Director of Women's Ministries, with as many as nine hundred ladies attending our events throughout each year. Pastor Bob McGougan was a strong leader, mentor and friend. As the overseer of the women's ministries zone, I met with him regularly and learned so many indispensable leadership skills from him. An invaluable lesson I learned was to let go of the false sense of responsibility I had when no one was willing take leadership of an event, a group, or a ministry. That it would 'die' was not my responsibility.

Today, I will often remind my audiences that if we begin thinking "Hey, someone should start a group like this" or "Our church should have a ministry that does that" or "I wish we could host an event for these" – it's probably the 'small still voice' of the Holy Spirit saying "*You* have been given a vision and *you* are called to make something happen!"

The most important lessons I learned at Pastor Bob's desk happened a number of years later. In the spring of 1998, after Jim had finally moved out to live with a girlfriend, I felt guilty about the deep sense of freedom and relief I was feeling. During a counseling session with Pastor Bob I said it felt as though a huge weight had been lifted off my shoulders. Pastor Bob explained something I have never forgotten: "Hope is the weightiest of all emotions!" The release or freedom I was experiencing was because

I'd let go of the sense of false-responsibly I carried in my marriage; the burden I'd assumed was all mine. I chose from that moment on to let my hope rest in God alone! I arrived at an important place of believing God could handle it all far better than I could anyways! LOL! Oh, the freedom I found in His forgiveness and love! So many lessons learned! I thank God for *Christian* counseling!!

These will be great bullet points for my next book, Charlotte Reed! LOL! I think it will be called "Abundant Living For Dummies Geniuses! LOL!

- "Letting Go" – a daily decision to let go of my expectations and my need for control. Letting go of the challenges of an unknown future while letting go of my fears… Letting go of stupid stuff… baggage… etc. etc
- "Letting God" – fight my battles for me!! Letting God lead me as I walk in the fullness of His plans and purposes for my life! Letting God be the ROCK – the foundation of my everyday living! What freedom!
- "Living One Day at a Time" – so-o-o-o important! Making the most of this day! Living in the moment!

Another powerful song comes to mind, ***Broken Love.***

Broken, the silence is broken.
As I read in His word He suffered and died,
His love I denied could save me.
Broken, the chains have been broken.
And the Lord gave to me a reason to be alive

Broken love He gives to you,
Broken lives He can undo
Broken dreams can now come true,
Behold the promise of the ages.
Broken love, Lord Jesus gave.
Broken hearts He came to save.
Broken lives can be remade,
His Broken love saved me

Gods' ways are not our ways! J<><

Since I have come to truly understand and embrace the truth of God's great mercy and grace towards me, I very deliberately try to extend that grace to others! Obviously it's not always easy, judging the hypocrisy of others was revealed as a huge stumbling block for me. When I was faced with my own hypocrisy, I repented and overcame it so now I have 'authority' over that beast! It's very straight forward, really!

I believe it's a choice. I've chosen forgiveness instead of judgment and understanding instead of unmet expectation. It's important to clarify that. It's the 'Jesus was not offended by me, so I am *not* allowed to be offended by them' philosophy!" That's something I learned from studying the book, ***The Bait Of Satan***, *by John Bevere*. It's the 'picking up your cross daily' kind of choice. I strive to love, to walk in acceptance and empathy and ask God to help me in that!

When someone hurts me or I'm especially discouraged in ministry, God reminds me of a few things He has already taught me. During the struggles faced in ministry, so often I've asked God, "Why? What's going on, Good Lord? Why are things not working? Why are the finances not coming in? The partners? The team? The invitations?" I've tried not to be impatient or frustrated or judgmental, even when I "know that I know" I'm doing exactly what God has asked of me and yet there is no response. Honestly, it's so hard and so dispiriting at times as Bob and I plod along at what I call 'the grassroots level.' We try to be obedient to 'press towards the mark' even though we feel so alone and so sincerely limited at times!

The 'living in a place of grace' principle or understanding gets applied when finances don't come in and projects aren't completed or bookings don't occur in the time period I feel the Lord had in mind. It has required learning to let go and, sometimes also means laying down the vision and plans I was so sure were right, even if just for a season. I used to wonder whether I had done something wrong or had been disobedient, but now I just sing "Grace, grace, God's grace" and remember.

One of my visions of Heaven puts it all into perspective very nicely. I've embraced it for the sake of my own peace of mind. LOL!

I am in Heaven, walking about with Jesus and it is a glorious place! There, suddenly opening up before me is what I think is the Tree of Life (or something) and as I look at the tree everything becomes so clear. I see many branches – the many projects and dreams God has for me. The twists and turns, the fabulous and vibrant life, the growth, and so many interesting contours revealed. A branch that was strong and vibrant has been sawed off. In that moment people became visible; their lives and their choices completely interwined with mine... Suddenly, before my very eyes, 'the branches' represent the many circumstances of our life together (Bob's and mine.) Also revealed is the sabotage of the enemy. I understand what happened. Unexplainable moments, I have pondered through-out the years, all clearly revealed. Whether ours or someone else's disobedience, rationalization, rebellion, or illness the bottom line is clear! So many 'unful-filled' endeavors finally make complete sense... A gazillion different reasons but knowing now it was God's own people who 'dropped the ball' 99.9% of the time. Grace flowing through me, I could see how so often there was nothing deliberate or sinister when potential partners and supporters missed the mark. Distractions and busyness had stopped the flow of 'life' in those branches... Clearly defined too, I could see how my own sin, weakness, generational and word curses had contributed to the sabotage of God's plans and purposes...

Wowzers! Sweet and beautiful grace! Flowing... flowing... and it's then possible to ask God to forgive them because they didn't really know what they were doing. Hmmm. Where have we heard that before, eh? Forgive me for my distractions! The revelation created a sense of humble self-realization as I said thank you, Lord, for forgiving us when we don't do what *we* need to do to help others fulfill their destiny purposes! I have prayed that the Lord will open my ears so I can hear His small still voice more clearly! Move me forward as your hands and feet extended! Let me be part of someone else's 'Plan A'! Oh, please, Lord!

I had absolutely no problem receiving this download, this revelation, because I'd had a few moments of discernment years before regarding my church ministry life. A precious and beautiful friend in the Lord had become the leader of the women's ministries department after I had stepped down from that role in the spring of 1998.

At the fall women's retreat, God had shown me that I was going to be the worship leader at what I thought would be the next district women's conference. I really didn't believe it at first and yet God had planted the seed so I was waiting. Even though I had enquired of the conference leadership, *nothing happened*! I began to think that maybe God was just testing me to see if I would be willing to do it. I really didn't understand it though. Months later, the phone rang. It was the sweet voice of my dear sister in Christ, Nettie Balzer, the director of Women's Ministries and she asked if I would consider being the worship leader at the upcoming women's conference. All I could say was, "OK!"

"I know you probably need to pray about it," Nettie said.

I told her that I most definitely didn't need to pray and that I knew God wanted me to do it. I felt Nettie was a bit dumbfounded until I explained that God had shown me almost a year before that I would be the worship leader at the conference. He had been preparing me for the job. Even during church services when I'd hear certain songs I knew they were the ones I would choose if I ever got to be the worship leader.

Nettie admitted that she had actually thought about me first. Instead she contacted another lady to do it, phoning her at least five times. She went on to say she just knew that this other lady was supposed be the worship leader. However, this other lady knew she wasn't supposed to do the job and kept refusing. LOL! Even though Nettie felt she was supposed to ask me, she kept shrugging it off because she was sure that I was just too busy. She proceeded to list off all the reasons and many ways she had disqualified me without ever asking me.

The crazy part was that the conference was taking place in Banff, Alberta where strict reservation deadline policies were in place. Since I was asked so late and close to the conference date, the registrations were closed and no additions could be made so I wouldn't be able to bring my usual worship team. Nettie said I would have to pick a team from all of the women who had registered for the conference.

God in his infinite and remarkable way worked it all out perfectly and knit the hearts of myself and another amazing lady together. A two-lady worship team! It might not have been all I'd thought it could have been, but it ended up working so well, it was obviously all God wanted and needed it to be at that moment!

Reflecting on these women's conference trips, I recall and extend a special thanks to another wonderful mentor, Judy McGougan. From her I learned to put a pillow down the center of the bed we shared. With this buffer between the two of us, we were not afraid of breathing or snuggling too close. Oh, and the snacks she packed! Between Judy and my blessed sister, Renae, I never felt a midnight craving.... not ever! LOL!

So you say you believe God is in control and has a plan for you but really, Lord? Bob? Oh, My Goodness!! LOL! J<><

Rebuilding my life as a single mom…, 'one day at a time, sweet Jesus!' and not doing too badly, I received a call at work. I was being summoned to the principal's office at school. I was horrified and definitely not happy. Being taken away from work to deal with the situation was not good! My middle child was an angry young man with some very significant hurts in his life. As I arrived at the school and went into the office I immediately asked Zach what he had done to get himself into trouble. He told me to f--- off. At this, the tall gray-haired man behind the desk stood up and escorted him out into the hall. He told Zach that when he could be nice to his mom, he could return and continue the conversation. After the door shut, I burst into tears. I was so upset and so concerned for my son. More importantly, I was worried about how his life would evolve when he obviously was having difficulties already. Although it should really be Zach's story to tell, I felt he had been brutally betrayed by his dad who was now way up north somewhere with another woman and couldn't even be found. The kindness and care of this principal were so touching it was like hope being extended to myself and Zach.

That day became memorable and strategic when, while waiting for Zach to return, the principal, who had introduced himself as Robert Faith, started sharing his story about having gone through a tough divorce and having a child that hadn't reacted well to it either. He shared how he hadn't given up on his son and he certainly wasn't going to give up on my son either. Bob saw the potential in Zach. He shared how he worked to make some changes in his life and how he labored to make good things happen for him and his son. Since he wasn't going to give up on Zach, he encouraged me to also believe in him and stand behind him. I needed to replace anxiety with trust! It was a *wow* moment! Bob even went so far as to tell me that the reason he was living in Medicine Hat was so his son, Reagan, who had completely turned his life around, could go to college there. More importantly, through his experiences he was able to minister hope to me about the future. During this discourse Bob probably sensed my loneliness and asked if I had other single parents as friends, which I didn't. He offered to be there for me if ever I needed someone to talk to and over the next while, we became very good friends. I would call him for coffee and it was helpful since he would tell me stories about other families who had survived marvellously. This wasn't the first time he had dealt with hurting families. Bob's words of encouragement from his own experiences truly helped me believe in my kids and a better tomorrow for each of us.

Bob and his son had been attending Victory Church in Medicine Hat, but the congregation was quite small. Pastor Len Thurman and Charlotte were great leaders and Bob loved it there. It was a charismatic, spirit-filled church, which Bob felt very blessed to be a part of. He was inclined, however, to move over to Hillcrest Church, which offered much larger and more active youth, college and career-aged groups for Reagan. Attracted by the fact that 250 kids hosted their own morning worship services, they ended up switching and going to Hillcrest on Sunday mornings.

Bob and I frequently got together after services. We'd go out for coffee and spend hours talking. We were also part of the high school's parent council and spent time getting to know one another there as well. On occasion we went out for supper together. From there the romance just seemed to blossom and grow and develop. When Charlotte asked if Bob was attracted to me the first time he saw me, Bob said probably not because that was when my son was in his office. He says he definitely noticed me during the months that followed because I was attractive and caring. LOL!

Over the next year and a half, by talking on the phone for hours every evening we had free, or visiting over coffee at the Steamin' Bean, I got to know about Bob's life and family!

His dad (Percy) and mother (Peggy) were married when they were only 18 and 19 years old, respectively. He recalls that his dad was about 6'7" and weighed about 290 pounds (a rather large man) and his mother was about 6' tall. This totally explains Bob's muscular build! Percy was enlisted in the army, so he spent a fair amount of time in Wainwright, Trenton and various other stations in Canada. In fact, he spent 35 years serving with the army in Egypt, Korea, Germany and several locations in Canada and Europe. As was the case with most military families, the mother was left alone at home to work and raise the children.

Bob was born in Calgary one and a half years after his brother, David. Peggy worked at Bell Canada, but life was a challenge being at home alone with the kids at night so she tended to enjoy going out partying with friends. It wasn't uncommon for her to abandon the boys for a whole day or even an entire weekend. This would get reported to Social Services at various times and Percy would come back for a while. Soon he would get called back out for maneuvers, and back and forth it would go. Social Services eventually decided that the boys should be put into foster care. Peggy's parents were somewhat old to raise children, but Percy's parents would not allow their grandchildren to go into foster care. So in 1952, the boys were picked up and taken to live in the Nipawin area of Saskatchewan where Bob's grandfather had homesteaded since 1928. Thus, David Sr. born in 1908 became known as "Dad" and Reddy, born in 1905, as "Mom". They cared deeply for the boys and made sure they had every opportunity in life. The boys' elementary school days were spent in Garrick and then they attended high school in Choiceland.

David Sr. wasn't involved in sports growing up as he had left home at the age of 12 to work. He wanted the boys to have that opportunity, so even though the farm took up a considerable amount of time, Bob's grandpa made every effort to ensure the boys got to play hockey and base-ball. This was so important to him that he thought nothing of getting up and onto the tractor at four o'clock in the morning in order to be done in time to take the boys to their sports. Maybe this is one reason Bob gets irked with parents who claim to be too busy to take their kids to ball or other sports-related clubs.

The only recollection Bob has of his real mother is seeing a picture of her in a red dress. He doesn't think that he would have recognized her if she had walked into the same room. Bob's dad, Percy, occasionally visited the boys and his parents at the farm in Garrick. Generally, he visited at least once a year and sometimes twice yearly in order to be there for Christmas. One of those visits is vivid in Bob's mind. He remembers that he and his brother weren't listening and behaving very well. His dad tried to step in and mete out discipline. That was a huge mistake! It wasn't often that his mom (really grandma) lost her cool, but she sure did on that occasion. She told Percy that he had no business butting in as the kids we're now their responsibility!

Bob excelled at baseball. He became so well accomplished that when he graduated from grade twelve, his first year of university was spent in the United States on a baseball scholarship. His childhood friend and roommate, Dave Pagan, continued on in the states to play professional ball with the New York Yankees for a number of years. Bob returned to Saskatchewan to pursue his degree in Education at the University of Saskatchewan.

A lot of Bob's success in baseball can be credited to his Uncle Ches who had never married and lived at home on the farm in Garrick. Bob says his dad was a great ballplayer, but he thinks that Ches might have been even better. He has fond memories of playing catch every night with Uncle Ches. This attention in combination with his dad's having him involved in baseball grew Bob into a fabulous player with an intense love for the game. He is still an avid baseball fan today and plays ball during the winter months when he and I reside in Arizona.

It is believed that Bob's biological mother, Peggy, died in about 1981. His biological father, Percy, passed away in 2011. Bob has two half-brothers and one half-sister from Peggy. His half-siblings tell him that Peggy was a pretty good mother to them most of the time; however, she would occasionally snap. When asked about this, Bob said he truly believes that his mom was not purposely neglectful of her children. He thinks it was mainly due to just being immature. The cause of her death turned out to be a brain aneurysm and the family and doctors wonder if she had it for many years. At the time of her death she was only in her early 50's. For this reason they wonder if it wasn't the brain tumor that caused her irresponsible behavior.

After living a good life and working extremely hard, David Sr. passed away in 1988. Reddy passed away in 1978 due to fluid on her lungs. The family believes she should never have died so soon. When taken to the hospital in Nipawin with fluid on her lungs she should have been sent to Saskatoon immediately. Instead, they spent time watching her to see if she got worse. By the time she did get to Saskatoon she had a stroke. They were able to stabilize her, but due to pressure on her lungs and circumstances she experienced another stroke and died.

Throughout Bob's last two years of university he dated a girl from the Loon Lake area named Elaine Weiers. After he finished university, they got married and moved to Regina where Bob finished his degree in Education at the University of Regina. They decided to move back to Bob's hometown of Choiceland, where Bob taught physical education for four years.

With Bob's leadership skills and wisdom he transformed the Phys Ed program at that school. He was able to improve the program so drastically that both the girls' volleyball and boys' football teams successfully competed at the provincial level.

During these years, Bob made the life changing decision that still guides his life today. There was a Mennonite fellow, Wally Dyck, with whom Bob taught. Wally loved to go golfing (even though he was a terrible golfer). He often invited Bob to join him. It totally amazed Bob how Wally never swore while golfing and Wally was always sharing the Gospel with him. In July 1978, while golfing on the nine-hole course in Nipawin, Bob decided on the third hole that he was going to give his life to Christ. The other man who was impacting Bob's life and joined them golfing was Jim Gregor. He was the Director of the Torch Trail Bible Camp where the family went every second Sunday for family church. So that night, at Torch Trail Bible Camp, Bob knelt down by the campfire, along with Jim Gregor, and dedicated his life to the Lord.

After four years in Choiceland, Bob decided it was time to move on. He had received an invitation for a promotion in Flin Flon, Manitoba. It also seemed like a good decision because sometimes it was hard to work in the limelight in a school where he had been a student for many years. By this time Bob and Elaine had two children. Jackie graced their home first, followed by Matthew. They were privileged to attend the little Baptist church just down the street from where they lived. Bob spent his days teaching and leading the physical education department at Hapnot Collegiate for three years. While they were living in Flin Flon, another son, Reagan, blessed their home. After another three years were spent in Flin Flon they once again decided to move.

It seemed hard to stay put and life was a constant series of moves. From Flin Flon they moved to Roblin, Manitoba where Bob spent one year teaching and was vice-principal in the grades 8 to 12 school. Their next move was to Ogema, a small town south of Regina, Saskatchewan. Bob worked as principal in the little school there. At this time another son, Andrew, blessed their home.

Elaine had grown up in the St. Walburg/Loon Lake area and they had always missed the trees and beauty of the northern part of the province. They moved up to St. Walburg where he worked as principal in the school there. During the ten years spent there the kids grew up and completed high school.

In 1993, the twenty-year marriage that Bob and Elaine had came to a halt. It is so easy to slowly grow apart when each partner gets involved in his or her own activities and less time is spent on the relationship. Bob describes it as the story of God taking a rope of two strands and joining them to make it a rope of three. Over time however, because of busyness and disappointment, selfishness and discontent, the rope breaks down and once again becomes two strands. Eventually those two strands are again single strands. Each of the people, become involved only in their own interests and desires. Although this was the truth as Bob sees it, he is the first to say there are no excuses for his resulting infidelity and destructive behaviors, but the end result is divorce.

When the marriage broke up Bob moved to become principal at an inner city K – 7 school in Yellowknife, North West Territories. Fortunately, by this time the kids were pretty much grown up and out on their own. Jackie and Matthew were attending the University of Saskatchewan. Jackie was pursuing a degree in Education and was playing with the U of S Huskies basketball team. Meanwhile, Matthew was working toward a degree in Mechanical Engineering. Reagan was an above-average student, but he was struggling since the divorce. He was hanging around with a group of kids that had little interest in school, rebelling to some extent and often quitting school. Having quit school himself, Reagan did go back and passed only one class out of four. Bob took him out of school in St. Walburg and put him in school in Yellowknife and after one and a half years he completed grades 11 and 12. Bob's youngest son, Andrew, remained in St. Walburg during this time.

The important thing to note is that Bob loved all of his children very much and always wished the best for them. Bob looks back on his life and he says he is much different now than he was thirty years ago. Back then he was much less sensitive and less understanding and probably less emotional. He knows his kids love him but, if he had it to do over again, he would give more hugs and less sternness. Yet if you asked Bob's sons, they would tell you the sternness and consistency were what made them strong. There also would have been more times of saying "I love you" and "I am very proud of you". Bob admits that his expectations of his kids were very high.

A humorous story Bob shares about his teaching days relates to the fact that he taught in so many different towns and schools during his career. While he was teaching in St. Walburg he and a buddy went to a convention in Saskatoon. They checked into their downtown hotel by the Midtown Plaza. At the front desk the girl said, "Mr. Faith, how are you?" When they got up to their room his buddy asked who that girl was and Bob told him it was a student he had taught in Choiceland.

For supper they headed out to a little Chinese restaurant on 22nd Street and Idylwyld Drive. They walked in and sat down. The waitress walked up and said, "Oh hi, Mr. Faith, how are you?" Again Bob's buddy asked who she was and Bob told him she was a student he had taught in Flin Flon. His buddy knew he had taught in Ogema as well and wondered aloud if there would possibly be yet another girl from there. After supper they were in a little sports store when a girl walked up and said, "Mr. Faith, how are you?" His buddy asked, "Where is this one from?" Bob replied, "From Ogema." LOL! Later as they walked back to their hotel, his buddy said, "Do you know everybody in Saskatoon or what?"

When Reagan was ready to transfer into college, Bob applied for and received a job as principal in Dunmore, Alberta. They relocated from the north to the Medicine Hat, Alberta area. Bob was especially blessed to be able to see his youngest son, Andrew, more often. On weekends the first year and then Andrew also moved in with Bob and went to school in Dunmore.

A SURPRISINGLY SPIRIT-FILLED LIFE! A
FUN AND FABULOUS NEW LIFE! J<><

Attending church events and activities had been a huge part of my life during the five years I'd been in Medicine Hat. Getting to know Bob meant sharing times with him at church. Although he and Reagan were also attending Hillcrest on Sunday mornings, on Wednesday evenings I began attending Victory Church with Bob. One of the things that I had never seen or understood before was intimacy with God, and that is exactly what Bob exemplified for me. He would literally weep during worship services and I knew I wanted that kind of closeness with God. Bob would walk across a room to share a 'message from the Lord' with someone. He could tell many stories of how he was used by the Lord to speak to strangers and friends alike.

His passion, as he shared his testimony, created a desire in me to be more tuned into 'listening' for the leading of the Lord. Bob told a story of how God used him to pray for two fellows one night at his church in Yellowknife. As they came into the service, God told him to pray for them – until they either went up to the front for salvation or until they left the church! Bob obediently did so… praying and praying until finally the one fellow went up to the altar. Bob starts weeping as he remembers feeling 'God's heart of compassion' for the man. He said he felt as though he could feel just a portion of God's joy as another soul was saved. BUT, Bob said, as his tears begin to flow even more, as he continued praying, the other man got up and left the church! Tears flowing, Bob recounts how he could feel God's hurting heart for the fellow who denied him that night!

I felt like a student sitting at the teacher's feet as Bob shared his experiences. He knew he was called to be an intercessor even though he thought the idea was laughable! God must have a sense of humor, he said, because Bob thought he was the least likely candidate to be an intercessor. However, one night God woke him from a deep sleep and said – you pray for your children! He began to pray… deeply, in the spirit he prayed, not sleeping for a few hours, until finally feeling released from his need to pray. The next day his son, Matt, called to say he and Jackie had been in a car accident the night before, unhurt only by some sort of a miracle! The back wheels and the entire axle of the car they'd been in, had been completely ripped off during the incident!

Attending church one Wednesday night with Bob, I was completely immersed in the worship, crying out to the Lord. I wanted to be free to worship as freely as Bob did, I wanted to go deeper and experience everything God had for me. Standing beside him, worshipping together, I realized Bob was speaking or praying 'in tongues.' As the realization came, I immediately recalled the conversations I'd heard throughout the years where people debated whether 'tongues' were for today, whether they were even okay or real or whatever. I realized what I *knew* about tongues was that the Bible said they should always be interpreted. As Bob was speaking in his heavenly language I suddenly began to weep. Hearing the words and the interpretation of them, I understood so clearly, Bob was simply and beautifully declaring praises to the Lord: God, I praise you… Father, I bless you… on and on. It was so beautiful and the experience profoundly impacted my heart, soul and mind as I felt so in tune with the Holy Spirit. Throughout the rest of the service, I felt a sense of peace, rest and contentment flow through me as I said over and over to the Lord, "I just want more of you, Lord… more of you." When the speaker was about to close the meeting, he said, "If you want more of what the Lord has for you, please come forward!" I almost bolted to the front! LOL! As he prayed over me, I felt myself floating backwards into a time of complete refreshing… total joy! As I 'awoke' I found myself on the floor. Bob helped me to my feet and told me to just start thanking the Lord… praying 'in the Spirit'. As I did, I realized I was now 'speaking in tongues'. I came to realize I had been 'slain in the spirit' and had received the baptism of the Holy Spirit with the evidence of other tongues. It was one little "ticka ticka ticking" type of sound and seemed almost silly, but Bob said, "Just use it to pray, especially when you don't know how else to pray… and relax! It's all good!"

Bob was also the reason I started my music ministry because he actually knew long before I did that I was meant to be a singer. When he decided to ask me to marry him, he knew he would make it conditional that I sing at our wedding. The Holy Spirit had shown him that I was supposed to be singing!

He planned for us to set up his mini Christmas tree on the evening of November 30th. I kept saying I needed to get home, but unbeknownst to me, Bob had a scheme to ask me to marry him when the clock struck midnight on December 1st (his birthday). As he presented me with a beautiful engagement ring, he said my yes would be the best present he could have, second only to twenty years earlier when Reagan had been born on his birthday. I accepted his proposal with joy!

Finally back home, as I lay down to sleep early that morning, I pondered my acceptance of his proposal and felt sick to my stomach. Looking at the amazing one-carat diamond engagement ring Bob had chosen for me, I still had to swallow my fear and trepidation. I knew I was attracted to him and loved so many things about him, but really I was downright overwhelmed and frightened! I realized I didn't believe in the whole 'happily ever after' thing anymore at all!

Instead of freaking out, I knew I needed to simply rest in the fullness of my belief that God had everything under control! That He did have a plan for my life, and *yes*, being remarried was really part of it! Laughing out loud, I couldn't help but remember there was a whole other crazy way to look at this relationship and whatever might end up happening with the two of us. First and foremost, although he was *not* someone I'd typically be attracted to (I'd often thought if God was going to have me remarry, a 'long-haired, bass-playing musician' might be the perfect fit for me... LOL!), I couldn't imagine *not* having him in my life!

Really though, a vision I'd had years earlier came back to me. It had popped into my mind two years before, the very first time I'd met Bob and I'd refused to go there! Now though, in the quiet stillness of the early morning, I prayed and asked God to give me the 'peace that passes all understanding!' As I took a deep breath I remembered...

In the early 90's, stuck in my marriage to Jim Barg and forbidden to sing, I was newly baptized and desperate to begin living a better life. I was depressed and 'loaded', having 'toked up' as I usually did each evening after the kids were off to bed. Suddenly I began having a day dream – an open vision -- As I stood behind the curtains I heard the voice of the announcer say "Ladies and gentlemen, Jodi Faith!" I stepped out from the curtains! As I walked to center stage, the applause subsided and I began to sing a beautiful and powerful 'God' song..." I remembered saying to God through my tears that night, "Am I going to sing again? Am I going to be able to sing for you again?" I had assumed it meant I would simply be changing my name! I had been reminded of that vision the first time I'd met Bob in the office that day with Zach. I had actually felt almost sick back then for just a minute, but I remembered very deliberately thinking, "Don't panic...perhaps he has a brother, or cousin or someone you'll meet through him!"

As my stomach flipped revisiting the vision... *"Jodi Faith!"* I laughed out loud into the glowing light of dawn! Thinking back over the last couple of years, my fears dissipated as I realized God did have a plan for the two of us to be together. He had begun to knit our hearts together and would continue to do so. I realized it might not be easy. We both had so many hurts and hang-ups and so much baggage! In spite of all that, the one thing I was sure of was that when life would be at its toughest, a great solace would be the fact that I knew God had orchestrated our lives, our meeting and our marriage. I took a deep breath and rested in that knowledge!

Bob became my cheerleader and number one fan! I had sung in choir originally to be supportive to my friend, but the music had a way of touching the depths of my heart especially when I was going through the rough waters and times of healing. Even though Bob didn't attend choir he was enthralled by my voice and claimed that he could pick it out over and above the other voices. He constantly pestered me and asked why I didn't sing any solos.

Even if I did want to sing solos I felt it was something beyond my ability. Solos had to be memorized and I had no memorization skills. Due to all of the years of drug and alcohol use, my brain had been affected greatly, and I suffered anxiety that I would forget the words during a performance so I refused to even consider it.

However, when Bob asked me to marry him on the condition that I sing at the wedding, I knew I had to find a way to overcome my fear. Since the choir was going to be doing a cantata for New Year's Eve and a soloist was required, I decided to audition. The music pastor immediately accepted me without any question. The song, ***The Potter's Hand,*** became a song of prayer and intention, praise and declaration for me over the years that followed as I gave my gifts and talents to Him!

> *Beautiful Lord, wonderful Savior*
> *I know for sure all of my days*
> *are held in Your hand*
> *crafted into Your perfect plan...*

Bob wept as I sang. He had noticed that I definitely had a gift to sing, but felt I wasn't using it. I made a decision to at least try, fear of memory loss aside! Laughingly, he says, "She still struggles with memory issues to an extent. She may have trouble remembering where her car keys or purse might be, but over the last fifteen years, God has given her back the ability to sing and memorize the lyrics of all her songs. It really is amazing that after not singing for over seventeen years, and in spite of all the drug and alcohol abuse, she is able to sing today. People who drink, smoke pot and cigarettes often lose the ability to sing." Bob goes on to say, "The way we know there is a living and powerful God is that she has been restored. The Word says the enemy kills, steals and destroys but Jesus came to give us abundant life! The Bible also says He'll restore the years the locust has eaten! God provides what He needs in order to use us. In Jodi's case, the gifts and talents He originally gave her have been restored as she has dedicated them back to Him for His use.

Bob goes on to say, "Would she be a better singer if she had continued to sing for those seventeen years? Who knows? But some of the things she is able to portray, she wouldn't have been able to do. Jodi's a great conversationalist! Her ability to feel for and understand other people and her sensitivity towards them was developed through the experiences and circumstances she has survived. The things she went through have given her a greater capacity for compassion and transparency, extending hope and wisdom as well."

Bob thinks about other people he has met. He says a couple of them can sing as well as or better than Jodi, but in his opinion, they do not have the same stage presence at all. He says, "Anybody can get up and sing and sound not too bad if they are a singer. There is a difference between somebody singing as entertainment and somebody singing as ministry. Whether a person is singing to a crowd of 50 or 500, when people can go home at the end of the night feeling the singer sang and spoke to 'them' and ministered to 'their needs' then that is a sign of totally captivating the audience. That's what Jodi does!" Bob feels that the seventeen years without singing and all of the drug and alcohol abuse have given her the ability to personalize her presentation in ways most people would never be able to. He believes her music ministry is a God-given talent. He feels there are many different talents and we all receive them from God. It is what we do with that talent that counts. When we use them to the fullest, it is our gift back to Him."

As I read Bob's words above, I'm reminded of how he believed I was called to sing! What a blessing his encouragement was and is to me. I began to realize God had predestined us to be together so His plans for our lives would be fulfilled! A song, **Only God Could Love You More,** has continued to resonate in my heart since we were first engaged but it wasn't until recently I could sing it without crying!

I asked the Lord for someone and I always knew
That in God's time and in God's way
It would be someone like you.
All my hopes and all my dreams were suddenly fulfilled –
it's almost unbelievable – our love was in His will

Only God could love you more
For He gave me this love I have for you
And what a blessing to know He's your Lord
'Cause only God could love you more than I do.

I'm tempted to be saying that we met by chance
But God was there at every step and in every circumstance...
To share this life God gave me seemed such a fearful task
But every moment we have shared is more than I could ask

The encouragement, blessing and heartfelt prayer of our closest family, friends, pastors and church family were contagious! Bob and I "Let Go and Let God." He was moving us into a new chapter in both our lives.

Ours was an absolutely beautiful wedding. On February 18th, 2000 the tables were set. White linens, black floating candles glowing in their beds of glittering crystal, red cinnamon hearts sprinkled across the tables, black linen napkins… Over two hundred guests gathered to celebrate the best day of the rest of our lives! Most wonderful was being able to seat our guests at the candlelit banquet tables! The reception hall was inviting, welcoming and intimate. We offered sparkling punch and appetizers after the moving ceremony and our friends and family began to celebrate while Bob's colleague took us away for photos all within the beautiful, warmth of Chinook Village. No need to venture out into the cold. Everyone's favorite memories include both my nephew Spencer and Bob crying like babies as I honored my beloved's request and sang my version of Chantel Kreviazuk's **Feels like Home to Me**! (I'd written new lyrics for one of the verses.) The song was a moving tribute to the hope we had found with a 'second chance at love.' Although it was a song that might not promise 'happily ever after', it was a song that spoke deeply of the future I had come to envision with him.

Blended family bliss? Oh, God help us!!!
This is more like "family in a blender!!" J<><

Bob believes the old adage that opposites attract because he was more 'old school' and more strict whereas my home was one with fewer boundaries and such. Newly married, it was an interesting time of life in our home when we ended up having five kids between the ages of 13 and 19 under one roof (my three and Bob's youngest two). Bob was about as different from me as night can be from day, and there were times of horrible conflict in our home in the early days of the marriage. Bob was not willing to let things like swearing or disrespect slide while I'd made the decision years before to pick my battles.

Simple examples of the type of things we had to work through included everything from routines (or lack thereof), Sunday morning church, laundry habits, cleaning and organizing the garage and setting budgets! The differences in how the kids were raised became very apparent as Bob's college-aged son had a curfew and my ninth-grade son did not! The fact that I married the principal was an interesting challenge and created many other issues, especially for my boys.

One day soon after the wedding, my brother asked me how it was going. I said, "Oh, Jason, please pray! We just need to pray. We're praying for blended family bliss!" Jason quickly replied, "And instead you've ended up with family in a blender!" LOL!

Our married life settled into a routine of my choir and worship practices, kids' events and our work schedules. The vibrant social life I had had as a single mom continued as we opened our home to friends. I had created a beautiful home for my family and when we decided to merge households, Bob built a fabulous master suite and an indoor hot tub room addition. With my passion for interior decorating and staging, we opened our home as a 'decor, antiques and collectibles' business. Faith House was created and I often hosted home shows and enjoyed these opportunities.

One of the deep desires of our hearts was that we would have the opportunity to minister together. When we were dating, Bob sang in a men's chorus while I sang with them as the descant voice in a ladies' trio. We loved being able to minister together so when my dad invited Bob to join Gideon's International, we were excited by the opportunity. The regular monthly meetings would be an opportunity to work and pray together for the Kingdom of God. Just days after we returned from our honeymoon, Bob joined the Gideon's in Bible distribution and pulpit fill. I joined the auxiliary and would sing during services where Bob would speak. We can look back and see how this was the beginning of the ministry God was growing for us.

Our blended family began experiencing times of 'bliss' especially during evening visits in the hot tub together! I suggest every family have one just for the purpose of gathering and chatting together – whether to begin or end the day – it's a great communication tool! LOL!

To the nations of the world? One step at a time! J<><

Opportunities started coming in for me to sing. I knew that God wanted my testimony told and it didn't matter where or to whom I was ministering, they would hear at least "one moment" from the story of Jodi Faith. I also learned that I was a storyteller and always sought to impart to others that they also have a story to tell. I feel society is full of people who have never heard of a loving and forgiving God, yet there are unending examples of how God has transformed lives! People are afraid to tell their stories. I feel Christians have to move from being an invisible army to being an intentional army, sharing personal testimonies every chance they get. The world will then know there is a living God Whom they can know intimately and personally, too.

God opened the door for me to begin ministering at the Drumheller Penitentiary. A regular monthly schedule was set and off we would go. I was praying about the whole thing knowing God was calling me to go, but really not understanding why. I had never felt much compassion for inmates or concern for them outside of wanting to see them receive the Word of God via Bible distribution with the Gideon's, but I knew I was being 'called' so was obedient to go.

I had been spending a good bit of time with my friends, Lynne and Roger Sabourin. Lynne was the wedding pianist and accompanist for my solo and other music ministry opportunities. One day, I felt the Holy Spirit telling me to call and ask Roger if he and Lynne would be willing to participate in the prison ministry with me. Immediately, Roger said "yes!" He also said he didn't need to pray about it because God had been showing him he was being called into prison ministry and so the team was born. Roger felt the Lord had been preparing his heart for years. He had a powerful testimony to share and the men responded very well to him. Lynne's ministry from the piano was powerfully wonderful, too! We were a great team together!

The remarkable thing about this ministry was how so many of the First Nations young men connected to me immediately. Although I had felt confused as to why God would want me to serve in this way, it was apparent almost at once! My testimony of drug and alcohol abuse and the domestic violence I had lived, put me into a place where the men thought of me much as they did their mothers. They opened up to me and shared so many stories of how they had grown up. Being an example of someone who had started life over in Jesus' name, encouraged the men to believe they too could begin again. They often asked questions about my children, finding hope for their own kids and their families, as I shared how we were all doing so well.

I was still employed in the family business where I enjoyed my position in marketing and promotions. The job had been a Godsend over the previous eight years and had allowed me to make a good living while setting hours that enabled me to be available to my children. As the years progressed though, the challenges of working with my mom became more difficult and at times our conflicts could be heard throughout the building. It bothered me deeply that our Christian example was so terrible at times. Most importantly, I began to worry about how the family could become fractured beyond repair if something didn't change. On a few occasions my brother and dad had mediated a peaceful solution to some of those conflicts, but I felt my time might be coming to an end there. I discussed my concerns with Bob over and over. Finally, after another argument, I broke into tears as Bob and I were rehashing the quarrel mom and I had that day. Bob said, "Jodi, it's not worth it! Just quit!" Feeling a sense of relief, I began to pray deeply about "looking for a sign from God" regarding leaving my job.

One day in church a promotional video was shared. The Youth With A Mission organization (YWAM) planned to bring their Impact World Tour to Medicine Hat to reach our city with the love of God. Drawing people from the highways and byways, YWAM introduced the hope of new life through forgiveness in Jesus' name. I felt captivated by the possibilities of being involved! They really needed committed workers! I began praying about how that would work! When I had been administering the Women's Ministries program in my church, the phone calls I took at my desk became another bone of contention between my mom and me. I knew God would work it all out if it was meant to be. I continued to pray.

It was only a few days later that 'World War III' broke out at work once more. This time it was outrageous! A terrible argument ensued. I called Bob from my desk bawling! He said again, "Just quit!" There was such finality to the thought, but I felt relief flood through me. I went to my brother and said, "Please, let me go. No more mediation; no more trying to fix things." Jason agreed. I said I'd come back in to train whoever would be taking over the administration of my marketing, promotions and customer loyalty position. With a good bit of fear and trepidation, I waited for my dad to come back to the office. I was prepared to have to work hard to convince him that I needed to go. You could have knocked me over with a feather when he arrived back at the shop, took one look at the two of us and agreed that my time there was done.

The next day I sat with my brother-in-law, Kerry, going over my job with him as he would be filling the gap I left. I rested over the weekend, and on Sunday at church was reminded of the YWAM project. First thing on Monday morning I called them and asked if I could volunteer. Given an appointment for that afternoon, I was asked to consider where I could serve best. Over the few years Bob and I had been married, I had begun feeling called into music ministry on a deeper level. I had attended the Breakforth convention for years and learned much about leading in worship and building my skill set. The conviction to serve in this way had grown. Bob's great encouragement always came with his belief that God had created me to sing more and more! As I pondered these things, I knew I would ask if there were any music ministry needs I might be able to help fill.

Arriving at the offices of YWAM, I prayed that the Lord would lead and that my availability to work would be a blessing to the entire project. I was ushered into a meeting with the staff director and local campaign chairperson. As they described their Impact World Tour I began to understand the project. An intentional strategy for outreach for the 'now generation', the crusade would be held over three nights, each showcasing different presentations and special guests. The Team Extreme was a group of power lifters with amazing feats of strength; GX International were bikers, skateboarders and hip-hop dancers and the Island Breeze would offer Polynesian dancers and music. Each event would draw uniquely different, yet interested crowds. They would ultimately hear stories about the living God each team member had come to believe in! As the campaign staff shared their enthusiasm and excitement that afternoon, I felt excitement brewing, too!!

Although it all sounded amazing and I felt strongly that God had closed doors so I could be there that day, I wondered how things would evolve. When the local chairperson asked how I felt I could help, I said, "God has been showing me I am supposed to be spending more time in music ministry. So to start with, I would ask if there is somewhere I could serve with music." The two of them looked at each other. Then the chairperson turned back to me and said, "We have all been praying and fasting since our staff meeting last week. We had determined together, as an organizational team, that we would not quit praying and fasting until someone came into this office and said 'they were called to serve as the Director of Music' for this campaign!" They went on to explain how they had approached all the music pastors and key music people in the city to participate! No one had been willing and yet here was Jodi Faith, unknown outside of her own church really, but sincerely 'called' to serve! They welcomed me with open arms.

Over the months that followed, I was also able to use my administrative skills to help the project in many other ways, but my most important duty was to build a team of choir members from all the participating churches in the city. These choir members would practice together and lead the partner churches in a prayer rally the day before the crusade began. I was blessed to be able to meet with pastors, share the vision for unity and build beautiful friendships among the ecumenical fellowship of believers gathered! YWAM said I had gathered the largest choir ever organized for an Impact World Tour.

The Tour was an amazing success with thousands of attendees dedicating their lives to the Lord. Many new visions for ministries and outreach events grew out of the spirit of unity that was celebrated during that time.

It was awesome! The financial support received was huge also, and while the local event was being planned, a new vision suddenly began to grow among the lead team – a vision to host another crusade, this time in India.

Each of the team members was asked to really pray about whether he or she was called to go to India! During the meetings and in the office, the invitation for this next event kept being mentioned! I was excited for those who knew they were to go, but I was *not* getting a sense that *I* was supposed to go. I continued to pray, but felt a bit of pressure to make a decision. I began to worry about whether I was somehow *not* hearing from the Lord. Anxiety began to grow. One of the considerations for me was the fact that I knew I was supposed to be focusing on music ministry now. Although I knew they needed administrators for the India campaign, I also knew there would be no music ministry opportunities. The pressure I felt to commit to go was growing and the deadline for signing up was within just two days!

I went out for lunch with my girlfriend, Sherry, and expressed my confusion and concern. I was in turmoil – really! My stomach was actually upset over the need to get an answer from the Lord! As we were leaving the restaurant, my friend suddenly said, "I think you and I should not quit praying until you get an absolute answer! You go home and I'll go home and we will PRAY!" I agreed and headed home. I actually got down on my knees in the middle of my living room and said, "God, I know you have a plan! I need to know it right now! Please!" Walking the floor, I continued praying and praying and praying and suddenly, the phone rang! The funniest part of the story is that I didn't know if I should answer the phone even though I was praying for an answer! LOL!

I picked up the phone and on the other end was a fellow from California! As he introduced himself, I was reminded that two years before I had submitted an audition to sing with the traveling ministry group called The Continentals. I said I remembered that audition, but why was he calling? "Well," he said, "we're putting together an outreach tour for this fall and would like you to join us!" Tears began to fill my eyes as he told me the dates of the tour! They were exactly the dates of the proposed India campaign. I knew God was closing the door to India and opening the door to tour the United States with the Continentals! Wowzers! I called my girlfriend and we laughed out loud! Our prayers were answered!

It was amazing how God had shown up at what seemed to be the very last moment! God's timing is always perfect! LOL!

The tour with the Continentals was unlike anything I had ever experienced. The opportunity meant I had to raise financial support as a self-supported missionary. With the wonderful contacts I had from across the city after the Impact World Tour, I had begun playing with a wonderful 'girl band'. They worked together with me to raise awareness and create a fundraising concert. Although the Canadian dollar was at its lowest point ever, all the finances came in that one night! I felt it was another confirmation from the Lord that I was to go! The music package arrived and I began practicing with anticipation of the tour.

When I arrived in Tucson, Arizona the rehearsals began. I was almost immediately singled out when the tour director asked if I thought I was smiling as I sang. "Well, of course!" I said. Nope, he said, I wasn't! I really couldn't believe it when he instructed me to stand in front of the mirror and smile, really smile, *while* singing! Not an easy task actually! LOL!! God began to show me so many other things I had no clue about as far as performing and being on the road – touring and praying for bookings! Boy, did I struggle to have grace toward the tour company over the fact that so few bookings were actually set as we gathered for rehearsals! I absolutely could not believe they didn't have a full tour schedule for us! Father, forgive me! Additionally, I learned about rooming with others, the ins and outs of set-up and take-down, the challenges of managing a cast and crew, the responsibility of the paperwork and financial deposits, and praying for the churches and fellowship groups we met along the way!

The most important thing that happened on the tour was how God broke my heart for his "family" and the small, struggling churches that stood alone in communities as a beacon of His light. In Utah, we sang in a tiny little church one night to only two folks! Here we were, a group of twenty-one – singing for two! I am ashamed to say I thought it was ridiculous! I struggled against the terrible spirit of judgment I felt towards the tour company again and this 'joke' of a church! God forgave me as I repented for my attitude later that night. I had discovered that those two dear saints (who were moved to tears by the presentation we had brought them) were the only parishioners left in their church. Persecution was rampant towards Christ-followers in the area. Children were banned from school sports and extra-curricular activities, folks were fired from jobs and businesses were boycotted if the owners or staff were members of any church other than the Latter Day Saints (LDS) in the area. My eyes were opened to the costs of being called into ministry, and to the blessings of ministering "where two or more are gathered" realizing God could mean this literally at times! Interestingly, it was after this revelation, repentance and commitment to go where God would open the doors that I had a vision of setting up and taking down "coffee house concerts." The dream included the vision of performing as a soloist and traveling on the road from point A to B. Ministering encouragement and hope to those I met, I knew many of the events were to be held outside the walls of the church building, too! Once back home, I felt an urgent call to create outreach events and to volunteer all the more outside of the church. I partnered with two sisters from the Catholic community I'd met during the Impact World Tour. Together we created Faith House, an outreach centre where we hoped the sale of Christian books, merchandise and refreshments would bring folks in. We dreamed of concerts and book clubs taking place there regularly and all shared the vision of being a place where Christian folk could invite un-churched neighborhood friends to gather. It would be a safe place for those choosing to live "clean and sober"! An alternative 'night-club' environment!

Me? Moving where?
Oh God! You can't be serious! J<><

As Bob began to approach his final years of teaching, he felt he'd like to move back to Saskatchewan to complete his career. The pension plan requirements (years of service plus age) would allow him to retire earlier and so he began looking for possible jobs there.

Originally, when Bob got the job opportunity in Lafleche, I thought I should remain in Medicine Hat for the first year. We would just commute back and forth to spend time together. After all, I recall thinking, there was no way God could do without me in Medicine Hat! LOL! I couldn't fathom moving to small-town Saskatchewan either. After much discussion and painstaking struggle, this plan actually seemed to be the way my future with Bob would go. That was until one day when he came home from work and declared that he felt like God was telling him that I was also supposed to move and be with him in Lafleche. I remained adamant that this had to be wrong.

Just as Gideon put out a fleece to seek God's answer, I put out my own fleece. That night I suggested we pray about the situation. We would put my house up for sale and we'd know it was God's will that I move if the house in Dunmore sold. Since the housing market was extremely poor and nothing was selling at the time, I was confident that my house wouldn't sell and I would remain there while Bob moved to Lafleche, SK. So it was agreed to put up a For Sale sign immediately.

In order to sell the house there had to be a few touch-ups done. Over the years paint had flecked off the exterior trim on the deck out back and the veranda out front, so they would have to be repainted. The plan was to start the project the next day after putting the sign out on the lawn. Bob was on the front deck painting and I was on the back deck doing the same. After only about an hour had elapsed, Bob approached me on the back deck and said there was a lady who wanted to look at the house. I told him I thought it would be best if she came back another day. However, the lady stepped outside on the deck behind Bob and said that she had looked at every house that was available in Dunmore the day before. She noted ours hadn't been put up for sale then! She said, "I know you won't understand this, but I am buying a house today." The lady was meeting her mother and sister later that day and desperately needed a house. To me, it seemed like the most inappropriate time since our kids had been home for the weekend and all the beds were stripped. Laundry was in progress and the floors were covered with piles of bedding waiting to be washed. The house was a total disaster area and now of all times this lady was saying she wanted to see the house!

I asked if she could possibly come back in an hour. That would allow time to tidy things up a bit to make the house more presentable and to clean myself up as well, since I had been painting. But the lady had no concern about the cleanliness and just wanted to have a look around. She wasn't taking no for an answer.

As I showed her around the house, I shared my story of how this house had become a sanctuary for me and my children. I also learned a bit about the buyer's story. The woman had three children and was in the midst of a nasty divorce. More mysteriously, her children were exactly the same age as mine were when we moved into the house. She was hoping maybe this house could be used to restart her life, anticipating a 'happily ever after' like the one God had provided for me. Looking at Bob she obviously was hoping for her own Greek God or something! LOL!

The house was sold less than an hour after she arrived! The fleece was showing that I was definitely moving to Saskatchewan with Bob. The only condition on the sale was that the buyer had to first sell another home in Medicine Hat. Her comments tugged on my heartstrings, as I'd been repeatedly seeing a vision of owning a rental property. The dilemma of selling her house in the city seemed to be the opportunity to fulfill the vision so I said, "Maybe I should just take your house in on trade!"

After discussing it with Bob and looking at her home in Medicine Hat, we decided it was obviously the perfect investment and a great income property. My best friend was going through a divorce and had a friend in the same circumstance. These women became my first tenants, moved in together with their children and found a true sanctuary of healing and safety.

Moving trucks loaded and knowing God was opening the door for me to move to Saskatchewan, I recall telling Him, "I will walk through any door you open, Lord!" Driving down the Red Coat Trail in my little white Volkswagen beetle car (which was smaller than some of the potholes on that road), I recall starting to sing a song that came to me suddenly... *"I found your glory on the Red Coat Trail... I found my destiny I found Your will..."* I began to panic saying, "Oh God, what are you doing? You know I don't sing country music!"

Pondering my upcoming new life in Lafleche I remember thinking too, how nice it was to have a fresh start! Bob was hired as the Director and CEO of the Golden Plains School Division. I felt his position was one of great honor and prestige and I remember thinking how nice it would be to just be his wife. No one would have to know of my sorry past... the brokenness out of my life of drug and alcohol abuse... Nope, I'd be starting over.

Just days after Bob and I moved into our new rental home in Lafleche, the phone was literally just installed when it rang. One of the local ladies asked if I would come to their weekly Ladies' Group to sing a song or two and share my story. "How do you know about me?" I asked. "Oh, we have family in the Hat!" was the reply. Swallowing the lump in my throat, I remembered my promise to God, that I'd walk through any door He opened. I met with those ladies and as Bob and I began attending church, we discovered almost everybody from our new Lafleche/Woodrow area retired to Medicine Hat. When transplanted folks attending the Faiths' church in the Hat heard that Bob had gotten the job and would be moving "back home", they called ahead to relatives and said, "You need to hear this girl's story! Have her sing and share her story!" LOL! "Oh, well. So much for keeping the secret!" I thought. Not long after, the phone rang again and again... I sang and shared at a couple of different small groups, telling little bits of my story and thinking that would be the end of it.

One of my passions is painting and interior decorating. In fact, my interior decorating business led to me being known as the Frugal Decorator of Faith House Antiques and Collectibles, our registered proprietorship. When we moved to Lafleche and into the teacherage owned by the school division, we weren't allowed to paint or change the interior. It was completely white which I found so-o-o boring. Bob asked the local handyman if he'd work alongside me to finish hanging curtain rods and shelves as his job had already begun at the division office. I busied myself unpacking and put my imagination to work to figure out ways to add color to the colorless world we were now calling home. I put dark brown curtains in the living room and some bright apple-green curtains in the kitchen (the perfect match for my strawberry dishes). Oma's old cupboard stood full of little treasures and boxes of extras were stacked in the partially unfinished basement for the day when we would move into a big house again! Once my new friend, Morris the handyman, and I had made the little 1,000 square foot house into a home, I sat there and wondered, "OK, now what, Lord? This is stupid! What am I going to do with my time?"

Our new little congregation would ask me to sing every so often and that was great, but not exactly fulfilling. Making meals and doing laundry didn't do much for me either quite frankly! One day the phone rang and it was our pastor. The church board had met and they were wondering if I would be the special guest at the annual Christmas party. I heard myself being asked to put together a Christmas program to present at this much anticipated outreach to the community. Asking what they had in mind, I was horrified to discover they wanted about a 'half hour or so' of music, then a break for dessert and games, and then a second 'half hour or so' of music. Since I didn't think I even knew a repertoire of that many Christmas carols I thought it all a rather scary venture. Add not knowing enough music to pull something like that off to the fact I'd need musicians, plus… plus… All sorts of fears assailed me, but again I remembered my promise to God that I'd 'walk through those open doors', so with great reluctance I said, "Okay." Praying like crazy about what I would do, I immediately went downstairs to a big box of music in storage. It had all belonged to the music department at Hillcrest Church in the Hat where I'd sung in a number of Christmas cantatas and pageants. Just before we'd moved, they had decided to begin purging much of their old music library. I had accepted their invitation to help purge and had taken a huge pile of these 'free' book sets (with CD's and cassettes) home. As I thought about this new project I knew one thing! The words of every song would be the most important aspect of the production. Reading through song after song I began to simply mark the pages of the songs chosen for their valuable, touching and inspirational messages; then I began listening to the songs on their associated recordings.

Looking back today, I can laugh out loud at how that first ever project came together. Perhaps because it was my first, it remains my favorite. It was the greatest project I've worked on because I felt God's presence as never before. I soon realized that I had picked songs that had incredible meaning and I would often weep while practicing their symbolic and moving lyrics. Interestingly, as I and my fledgling band began practicing, I still had no idea what the show would actually end up looking like.

GOD OPENS DOORS NO MAN CAN SHUT...
AND SHUTS DOORS NO MAN CAN OPEN! J<><

Toward the middle of November, Bob was scheduled for a Saskatchewan Education Conference in Saskatoon to be held at one of the most beautiful hotels in the downtown core. Bob had meetings in connection with his position as school division administrator and I decided I'd go along and use the time as a retreat, especially looking forward to enjoying the hot tub and swimming pool over coffee every morning. I would spend these few days totally focused on putting the songs into order. Praying throughout, I'd figure out how the Christmas show was to evolve.

Many things became very obvious to me during that retreat. Even though I hadn't seen things as clearly when it was happening, I began to see how God had to remove me from ministering in my church of one thousand people in order to prepare me to minister to the world. Any possible anxiety or fears were short-lived because I knew that when the fleece had been put out about selling our house in Dunmore, God had shown up indeed, proving He wanted me to follow Bob to Lafleche. Life had changed in a drastic way as I learned to trust and obey the Lord. Realizing God had a whole new plan for my life was awe-inspiring and humbling. That I would go from never having sung, to a solo in a New Year's cantata at Hillcrest, to carrying an entire show was downright crazy! I took a deep breath and exhaled slowly as I knew it was obviously God's will.

Thinking back, I realized how blessed I was that Bob had discerned God's will for our lives and that he had sensed God had something for me in Saskatchewan, something for the two of us together. As Bob and I traveled from Alberta to Lafleche it had become apparent to him that part of my resistance to the move was that I had to 'let go' of the security I felt in having a roof over my head. Throughout all the struggles and hardships, I had worked hard and had successfully rebuilt my life and my children's lives while maintaining a home. With the wonderful support of my family, it had been an awesome season, but in so many ways the move was like an end to my former life. Bob reminded me, "You have to learn to let go and let God. Don't you trust that I will provide for you and put a roof over your head? You have to let it go."

My retreat time in Saskatoon was amazing. God seemed to snuggle me very closely to Himself during the long quiet days of reflection. The motto at Hillcrest back in 1994 was LOVE, MEND, TRAIN & SEND. God was achieving His purpose for me even if He did have to literally pluck me up and move me physically to His chosen mission field. Hillcrest people had taken me in as a wounded sparrow, a broken old clay pot and just loved me. They prayed with me and for me, mentored me and cared for my needs. My healing journey and transformation were remarkable. Through the mentoring program, I became an apprentice mentor to others. The music arts and women's ministry circles that I had 'plugged into' put the LOVE, MEND, TRAIN & SEND philosophy into practice beautifully and effectively.

As I focused on the Christmas program and the message of the songs, I began to weep. I realized it was not only the story of Christmas, but also a story of God's great love for me. Telling Charlotte about that profound moment, I broke forth in song, *"Isaiah spoke the word..."* From the first song to the last, the presentation taught me that even before time began, God had a plan for me. And that plan was to bring me back to the heart of His love.

Going to a wine and cheese social with Bob on the last day of the conference, I looked like a wet noodle. I'd been moved to such a degree, I'd wept the entire day. Never had I been so intensely touched by God! This whole Christmas show was turning out to be a reminder to me that God had never once left me nor failed me. I'd not been forsaken or forgotten by the King of Kings and the Lord of Lords. It was all so overwhelming that at the time I really couldn't fully understand or realize what was happening to me.

Charlotte laughs as I break out into song again... **Bethlehem Star** is still my favorite song of all time. Even after performing this Christmas program for over ten years, it still remains intrinsically powerful. Its message reminds the audience that God continues to pursue us with His great love.

It seems that the world might have changed after all this time.
But people keep losing their way and choosing their own design.
It seems that the Lord might give up but He's true to the end.
He keeps calling our names and drawing our lives back to Him.

And the soft steady light of the Bethlehem star,
Keeps lighting our darkness and touching our hearts
Calling us back from wherever we are…
Back to the Father above,
Back home to the heart of His Love

No matter how far away from Him and His plans for us we are, He continues to draw us back to Him. I myself lived in a place of great darkness and had been carried into the "light" by the God who had loved me. A God who had shown himself real over and over – the one true living God – who'd partnered with me in a new life of hope, light and celebration! Awe-inspiring, humbling and worthy of more than "a few tears through the years" to say the least!

The response to the outreach at Woodrow Gospel Chapel during that first performance was so remarkable and encouraging. Bob read the passages from Isaiah to begin the show then wept throughout the entire presentation as he was so touched by the Holy Spirit ministering through the story portrayed. With my great band-mates, Ed Rigetti and Jackie Poirier, we took this program out on the road and did twenty performances the first year and thirty the next.

Having learned a lot during ministry, worship and performance classes I'd attended while at Hillcrest and Breakforth, creativity and theatrical input became important to me as I prayed over how best to present this Christmas story in the different venues. I feel there are often people who need to hear more than the music; they also need visual symbolism to draw them in. I realized during my journey that I was like this growing up. I was bored with Christian music most of my adolescent and early adult life. Therefore, pondering a new year of presentations, I decided the concert would begin in total darkness. I would walk down the aisle, from the back of the church to the stage with one lit candle as Bob spoke from Isaiah, **"The people walking in darkness have seen a great light; on those living in the land of deep darkness a light has dawned. For to us a child is born, to us a son is given: and the government will be on his shoulders: And he will be called: Wonderful, Counselor, the Mighty God, the Everlasting Father, the Prince of Peace.** Isaiah 9:6 (KJV) Putting the candle in its place of honor, I stepped onto the stage. You could have heard a pin drop before the music sound track began. I picked up the mike and sang, *Jesus You Are Him.*

> *Isaiah spoke the word... that a mighty one would come...*
> *To bring healing to all nations and restore Jerusalem...*
> *Many centuries then passed 'til the perfect time had come...*
> *Then a little boy was born as a lowly carpenter's son...*
> *And Jesus you are HIM!*

Reminiscing over that first amazing and dramatic presentation, I start laughing. Seriously! LOL! The entrance was so moving and then as I'm singing the words to this powerful first song, suddenly, I hear a voice calling out, "Jodi, we can't hear you. The mike isn't turned on." It was the voice of my dad calling out from the audience. A moving and unforgettable concert planned for my "sending church" in Medicine Hat and yet instead, one of those horrible, ridiculous, almost-too-funny-to-be-true kind of moments – LOL! At least I can laugh about it now, and why not? God graciously flows through these old clay pots and the Holy Spirit moves in spite of us! Even though I knew I'd blown it at the beginning of the evening, a lovely lady came up to me and complimented my choice of songs "Never," she said, "have I seen the Christmas story portrayed in such a touching and moving manner! And more importantly," she said, "I have always been so bored by Christmas songs!" Her heart had been totally captivated from the very first moment Bob's voice had begun to narrate and I had started to sing that night! "Oh, how I loved the unique songs! Not just the old carols, but also such new music!" She asked, "May I buy the album, please?" LOL! I was blessed to say the least!

After the second year of performing this Christmas show, Bob and I realized we needed to put together an album. A friend had a simple recording studio in his home in Lafleche. Jackie, Ed and I began working with him to produce a Christmas album celebrating the songs from this great presentation. The result was a fourteen-track inspirational Christmas album, including the bonus of two instrumental tracks by our friend, talented sound technician and flutist, Rhys Frostad! In December 2005, the pre-release of "Reflections of Love" was ready. My dear friend, Betty-Ann, joined in on a few harmonies, too! It was an awesome success and the show remains so all these years later.

Often, audience members have asked for the narrated version of the story which we did not have! They are always so disappointed as they feel their loved ones or friends would benefit so much from hearing the way I interject my testimony into the show. A DVD project was discussed many times through the years. As that vision grew, I began seeing it on television as well. I began to see visions of actors and people portraying the various roles. Excitement and anticipation growing, it just might be possible!

Praying about it, I would write down ideas here and there. Through the years that followed, I became the cantata leader where I sang and shared my story and the Sunday school kids sang along with me and acted out the parts. In Moosehorn, Manitoba, I did just such a performance and the tiny tots were dressed up like little sheep. Absolutely adorable! The seven to ten-year olds were the shepherds that tried to contain the two and three-year old sheep. Each shepherd had one sheep that he was to keep from falling off the stage. Cute and hilarious!

Participating in these kinds of community cooperation opportunities continued to grow the vision which has almost been realized. A collaborative project with Interlake Christian Films of Riverton, Manitoba had me filming my narrated Christmas show during December 2012 for proposed distribution to television, download and on DVD! All your prayers are appreciated, please! LOL! We are pressing toward a 2014 Christmas season release.

I KNOW YOU HAVE PLANS FOR ME, LORD, BUT REALLY?
I JUST WISH YOU'D GIVE ME A CLUE WHAT
THEY MIGHT BE! LOL! J<><

Settled into the monotony of winter after an exciting first season of Christmas concerts, once again I was bored to tears with my life in Lafleche! I felt the Lord saying, "Get your house in order!" so I had busied myself getting everything absolutely organized! Work done, I'd been laying on the couch watching TV and wondering what I was going to do to fill my time. I was actually praying and begging God to do 'something' with me when the phone rang! I was intrigued by the interesting phone call. Sherry Sproule, the piano teacher in the local area, introduced herself. Cordial and gracious, she explained how her very talented daughter was involved in piano and voice as part of the local music festival community. Sherry said she and her husband had been very moved by my Christmas presentation and were especially interested to know if I would be willing to give Audrey voice lessons! I was actually dumbfounded by the request.

Bob returned home for lunch and I mentioned Sherry's invitation! I couldn't imagine it, really! Being a teacher to voice students? Bob, once again seeing life so much more clearly, said, "Why not? In fact, who better?" He went on to say, "You had ten years of Royal Conservatory Voice lessons. You have great stage presence and are a wonderful entertainer. Seriously, I think you should go for it!"

I called Sherry back and we discussed the idea at greater length. As we chatted the vision in my heart grew. Sherry was presently teaching over sixty students throughout Bob's entire school division. Many of these students wanted to participate in vocal classes at festival, but Sherry felt unqualified and limited by time constraints to really do much. If I were interested, I would create an invitation to be sent home with the children and Sherry would distribute it to her students.

I was reminded of how I'd told God I'd walk through the doors He opened, but I was deeply concerned about it all! As I began praying like crazy about the whole thing I had a great thought! (I had loved attending Breakforth through my years at Hillcrest. Our new little church in Woodrow was supportive of Ed and me traveling to the music conference together later that month!) I said I'd know I was meant to teach the kids (call it putting out another fleece) if I could just get into a few vocal sessions to renew my training skills.

Anticipation for another amazing weekend at Breakforth had begun! What in the world did God have in mind? Although I was already registered in a number of other classes including song writing and worship leadership, I'd know I was 'called to teach others' if I could switch from my chosen workshop sessions and get into the vocal track when I got there. My heart was resting on God's plans for me as I waited to head north.

As we traveled to Edmonton, I remembered my old friends from Hillcrest, the wonderful courses and many amazing moments we had shared at the largest worship conference in the nation. Again, I knew I needed to completely trust God for direction and wisdom as we arrived. Reminiscing about years past, I said to Ed, "If you really seek the Lord, He will show up here, brother!" We were excited and anticipating a great weekend!

First thing Friday morning, Ed went off to the first of his chosen courses as I quickly went to stand in line at registration. I walked up to the counter and discovered it was absolutely no problem for me to get into the vocal stream of classes for the entire weekend! My song writing course booked for that day was not going to conflict either which was cool. Off I went, knowing God was orchestrating my life. I was reminded of the scripture, **"For I know the plans I have for you... Plans to prosper you and not harm you. Plans to give you a hope and a future."** (Jeremiah 29:11 – NIV)

As I settled into my song writing workshop with Marty Nystrom, who wrote *As The Deer*, I felt blessed although inwardly I was laughing at the fact that I even thought I was called to be a songwriter. Marty entered the room to begin his session and as he passed me, he stopped and said hello. We visited just a little bit when suddenly he spoke into my life with words that brought tears to my eyes. He said, "God has put you in this room today because He has called you to be a huge blessing to many others through the songs you will write!" He smiled and headed to the front of the room. Marty began to speak as the room full of eager students "sat at his feet." As I listened, I wept! He then asked everyone to stop and ponder a few things... maybe a phrase or scripture that was important to them... and I wept! Blessed, but moved beyond belief I would laugh, then cry! All day, I wept. LOL! Another amazing weekend at Breakforth had begun! What else did God have in mind?

After an emotional day in my first ever song writing class, I was able to meet up with Ed at the large session held that evening. There was a sweet, sweet spirit in the place. As we were worshiping together, Paul Balouche was singing his amazing new song, ***Open the Eyes of My Heart, Lord***! As five thousand voices sang together, I turned to smile at Ed. I asked him how his day had been. Ed said it had been great! I then asked him, "So, what did God show you today?" Over the noise Ed laughed! He said, "He showed me you're supposed to sing country music!" "Oh, whatever," I laughed too! Ed said, "I'm serious."

I turned away as I smiled. Ed had been bugging me about doing country music ever since we'd started working together! I, of course, had made sure Ed knew I didn't do country! Ignoring him, I continued to sing, *"Open the eyes of my heart, Lord... Open the eyes of my heart, I want to see You... I want to see You."* Suddenly I stopped and began to pray. "Oh, Lord, please, let me hear You... let me see You..." Revelation came to me as suddenly I said, "Oh, God, please forgive me. If you really want me to sing country music – if I've been ignoring Ed and all along he was speaking for you... speaking into my life – oh, God, I'm s-o-o sorry!" I began weeping again! This time I was laughing, too, as I envisioned the look on my old voice teacher's face. Mrs. Mells had trained me to be an opera singer – what if all along I really *was* supposed to be a country singer? Oh, my goodness, I thought, Mrs. Mells was probably scared to death about my singing country music! Perhaps that's why she was always making snide comments about 'scooping' and 'swooping' like country singers way back in the day!!

I know it was a crazy, amazing pivotal moment although I couldn't possibly know how things would evolve. I just knew I did *not* want to stand in the way of whatever God was planning to do... in me, and to me and through me! Amen!!

Second Chance? To tell the truth, the whole truth
and nothing but the truth... so
help me God! LOL! J<><

That first season of Christmas concerts also led to invitations to return and present another concert in the spring. I began working with Ed and Jackie to create another song list. Interestingly, God started laying on my heart many of the songs that had been special to me through the years since I'd begun singing again (in choir and as a soloist). I asked my parents and Bob for their input to create the song list and my first album began to take shape. Praying over every step of the process, suddenly I remembered a song that I wrote twenty years earlier entitled **Second Chance**. I went to my newly organized music library! LOL! I pulled out the lyric sheet created all those years ago and at this point in time, I realized that this song was actually the story of my life and would someday become the title track.

I had experienced a vision twenty years earlier seeing this song as a music video. It involved an older woman listening to a little girl, who as they looked at a doll in the window, tells her story of homelessness. The woman realizes she must help the child and her family. Rediscovering this song, I was rocked as I realized it could have been an exact replica of my life story as told by my own little girl.

I prepared this song with Rhys Frostad who helped me finish it. As I share this story with Charlotte, I break into a gentle rendition of **Second Chance**:

"I'll remember that lonely day,
The lovely dolly that was on display...
The little girl who looked away
And through her tears began to say...
I used to feel just like that doll.
Warm and secure and loved by all.
I never cried, we had it all...
The folks and me, we stood so tall.
But what will be, will be, my mama told me so."

Now speaking, I finish the first stanza of the song,

She told the story of her life,
How her mama's suddenly a battered wife.
Pa worked so hard, but lost it all
He's amazed he ever dreamed at all...
Cuz what will be, will be; no second chance you see

Ed Rigetti and Jackie Poirier became wonderful friends as we practiced and worked together on our repertoire of songs! Called "The Full Circle Tour", they were willing to travel with me as I revisited a number of the communities and churches of my past. I went to each one and sought forgiveness for the times when I was judgmental or less than supportive to the people that God loved so much.

God had literally broken my heart for His Church. I'd learned how easy it is to judge hypocrisy in others and not see it in ourselves. I testified from a place of new understanding as I sang and shared! I sought forgiveness from these congregations because I'd realized I had no right to expectations of any church. "None of us have that right!" I said. "Our job is to go to church and be part of the solution and part of the love that is extended. We shouldn't be expecting others to love us."

The leaders of one of these churches, where I had attended for over 10 years, gathered around a table for an elders' meeting on the Monday evening following my concert there. The pastor went around the table and asked each of them to share how they had reached out to me and my children when we were found suddenly homeless and going through our rough time. The pastor asked how many of them had actually called me or asked how they could help. It was discovered that not a single one of those families had been there for me. As a ministry council, they wrote a letter asking for my forgiveness also. A huge stepping stone to greater healing in my life no doubt, and yet not something I would have ever expected to receive from them.

So I'm going to be a singer when I grow up, eh!? LOL! J<><

The reality was that Bob and I were going to go broke traveling and being on the road singing all the time without any funds coming in. People were asking for my music and we thought that would be a way to generate income but having CDs doesn't just happen!

I was involved in creating a huge New Year's Eve outreach event. I had met a fellow who ran a production company at a conference in Drumheller, Alberta, where I led worship. I had arranged for Gary to provide the sound and lights for this event although having him was crazy expensive. I was able to book the gym in Bob's old school. The plan evolved and I asked him to do a live recording that night. The next morning he would record three additional songs with my favorite accompanists, Lynne Sabourin and Juanita Faas. Friends of mine, Moe and Anita Palmier and Ed Rigetti also performed. It was a great night for the artists although the turnout was disappointingly small. The live recording from the evenings concert, turned out to be terrible but the three songs recorded the next day became the foundation of the **Second Chance** album. Another learning experience, LOL!

The music community in Saskatchewan offered invaluable advice and education to me as I began to live out the reality of having a fledgling music ministry. One day over coffee at a SaskMusic workshop, I began visiting with another delegate. Ruth Koop was well-versed in the music world, having worked within the music department at a local Bible school. Many of the local bands from the school had gone on to make music on a national and international scene. As well, Ruth had been involved in much of the paperwork and administration of their projects.

During conversation, she also mentioned that Briercrest Bible School at Caronport, SK had a recording studio and did projects for folks coming from off-campus. Interestingly, I had at one time dreamt about being at Caronport. Because Bob and I lived relatively close to the campus, as the crow flies, I'd thought I might finally be able to go to Bible school and had considered applying. No Bible school, but my first album **Second Chance** was completed over that winter with additional songs recorded at the Sound Tech Studios at Caronport.

On that album were a couple other tunes that have become fan favorites as well! After Ed's declaration that I was supposed to be singing country music, I waited on the Lord to show me how and when! I was almost immediately reminded of the song He had tried to give me all those years ago....*I Found Your Glory On The Red Coat Trail!* As Bob and I were on our way to Regina one evening, the song began running through my head again! On the super cool, brown paper tablecloth at Montana's restaurant, I wrote out the completed song lyrics. I took the song back to Lafleche where Ed and I worked it out!

I Found Your Glory on the Red Coat Trail,
I found my destiny, I found your will!
Kinda surprising it took leaving it all
To find your glory and to find my call!

The Woodrow Gospel Chapel allowed me to grow in the gifts and awareness God was giving me. Now acting as worship leader, my worship team and I were free to lead the congregation! One night when Pastor Randy and I were chatting, I told him how scary it was for me, as God was making me sing country songs! "In fact," I said, "God just gave me an awesome song called *Walkin' On The Water!* As I sang a few bars, we laughed together about how frightening it can be to *"get outta the boat!"* It was a couple of days later when Pastor Randy called and asked me how the new song was coming along. I said, "Well, it's actually sounding pretty good. Why?" "Well," he said, "I'd like you to sing it on Sunday! It looks like God wants me to speak on 'getting out of the boat' too! LOL!"

Oh, I coulda' been walkin' on the water, livin' the abundant life
Singing and dancing in the twilight, overcoming every fear and fright

Your power was so apparent, I shoulda' got up to my feet
Said I'm with you Lord, thru thick & thin. Together, I'm complete!

Oh, I coulda' been walkin' on the water, but I completely missed the boat
The abundant life you had for me, I feared it was a joke
But now I want to be dancin, singin… walkin' on the water with you
Wanna' praise you as my Mighty King, ain't nothing we can't do.

More than I ever dreamed or imagined Lord! LOL! J <><

As the album was coming together, my phone rang and I was told there was a man I needed to meet. He was trying to bring a homelessness housing strategy for men, to the city of Medicine Hat. Since I was traveling to the Hat monthly to stay connected with the girls who were running Faith House I agreed to meet the guy. It was a great meeting! Vision began to take life and I was very excited! I felt I was to come alongside this man and his very worthwhile charity. I could see myself touring on behalf of his organization, to create awareness for his project and help expand to have homes in across Saskatchewan and Alberta.

Homelessness and all that is attached to it was definitely something I knew about, even though my parents had stepped in quickly to protect and save me and my children. I knew what it felt like to have housing, security and everything else stripped away in an instant. Completely shattering! It was a psychological loss for me, since I wasn't reduced to living on the street or under a bridge, but I definitely knew what it was to wake up one morning with no place to call home. I knew what it was like to be battered by the storms of life and feel completely overwhelmed and helpless.

Becoming an advocate for The Champion Centre (CC) seemed a perfect fit for me and a great strategy for engaging communities. The "Where's the Love" Gospel Music Songwriters Showcase was born. I thought it might be neat to host songwriter circles in towns throughout the two provinces. The locals would become involved in a contest to see who wrote the best song on the Where's the Love theme. My prayer, as I shared the vision for the tour with CC, was that individuals at these concerts would grab hold of the CC vision and help make it happen in their cities, towns and villages!

Partnering with my friend and marvellously talented pianist, Juanita Faas, I prepared to go on tour and tried to get tour dates. I shared the vision with friends I met through SaskMusic and the songwriters group in Saskatoon under the direction of Jody Bryant. Aven Grace called to enquire about the tour. From Nipawin, Aven was a songwriter and member of the Saskatoon Songwriters. She and I had a meeting to answer a few of her questions. Aven was curious about what I was going to be doing at the Saskatoon event, since she was considering being involved there.

Putting a tour together proved to be very difficult. The May dates filled in okay, but it was especially tough to get a booking for the first week of June. After all, this was big time farming season. Another challenge presented itself as I learned that the traditional church pretty much shuts down by the long weekend of May and doesn't get back into full swing until October. Pastors would say, "Sorry, it sounds like a great idea, but trying to get people into church on Sunday is hard enough, let alone for a concert on the Tuesday night you have available!"

Alternatively, I would contact churches and pastors would ask, "But can you sing?" It didn't take long to figure out that there were gospel singers doing concerts that, according to these folks, really couldn't sing well at all. My credibility was being questioned because at this point in time I was pretty much an unknown entity. What I needed was some exposure so people would know Jodi Faith as a capable songwriter and singer. I remember praying and asking God for some sort of a newspaper review or something that would say, "This lady really can sing!"

WHAT IS THE COST? HMMM... REALLY LORD?
THIS IS A WAY BIGGER CHALLENGE THAN
ANYTHING I EVER EXPECTED! J<><

Discouragement set in as I had a full week during mid-tour with not one booking. I called my new friend, Aven, to see if she might have some contacts that might be able to help. After all, the tour was going to be up in the northeast corner of the province where Aven lived. I remember being totally caught off guard by Aven's immediate response! She told me she knew exactly why I couldn't get any bookings! She said she knew exactly where I was supposed to be! The Country Gospel Music Association (CGMA) of Branson, Missouri had scheduled their Canadian convention in Yorkton that *same* week. I thought that was no help to me since I didn't do country music, even though I had written songs like **Second Chance**, **Redcoat Trail** and **Walkin' On The Water**, which all had that country sort of sound to them: I DO NOT DO COUNTRY! I remember crying out to God!

Even though I didn't know if I really belonged at this CGMA thing, I sought the Lord's direction. By this point in time, my new rule was to "ask, seek and knock" and God would open the right doors for me. Promising Aven I'd follow through, I phoned the guy who was putting the event on and was shocked when I heard him say, "Jodi Faith! I've heard of you. What are you doing on the Sunday night? We are putting on a big concert to kick off the week and I'd love for you to be one of our special guests." LOL! "Wow! Thank you!" I accepted the invitation as a sign! "Thanks, Lord!" I said, as I penciled in the CGMA and continued to plan the tour! I was excited!

As I prepared to go on tour, Bob was totally stressed. As far as I was concerned, a concert tour requires sound and lighting. Gary was a great friend who had what I needed. He offered to go on the road with us for a certain fee, of course. Not knowing the ropes at this time, I just sort of rolled with it, but it seemed that at every turn there was more and more cost. Bob's anxiety was growing! However, the night before I was to leave on tour, Gary's mother was admitted to hospital for possible heart surgery so he wasn't able to go. The tour went on anyway and I made do with the sound systems in the churches where I performed, or systems borrowed from people in the community. Interestingly, everything was fine with Gary's mother in just a few days. From this experience, I told Bob I felt that God would always look after any money issues that we would face. Basically, God would open and close doors as He saw fit. Bob's concrete, sequential response was that we should never have had to worry in the first place and I should have been thinking more clearly. LOL! I, however, now gained the security of knowing that I should continue to press on and be obedient. In spite of my willingness to spend money or do whatever it took to get the job done, I knew God had protected me from my own ignorance and would continue to do so in the future.

Another thing that happened the night before the tour, is something that has continued to power our ministry in the many years since. As I was packing to leave, Bob said he wasn't at all happy about it! I said, "You started it all!" Bob replied, "I didn't get remarried so that I'd be alone." I said, "When you married me you knew it would always be "God first, you second". The battle ensued and finally Bob stormed off to bed!

I was sad. I continued to pack, but my heart was so heavy! Crying, I was upset. The fight had been brutal but worse, I was scared too. What if I had not heard correctly from the Lord? How could it be God's will for me if Bob was going to be so distressed? I remembered how soft his heart had been when we first met, how he usually responded to the moving of the Holy Spirit! How discerning he always was regarding the things of the Lord! "Oh, God" I cried out, "please, You have to do something! Soften his heart *or* show me what's wrong! Am I not supposed to go?" As I fell asleep, I thought about the fact that the "sun had gone down on our wrath" and my heart hurt!

It was 4:30 the next morning as I quietly got up and prepared to head out to Swift Current for a meeting with the ecumenical ministry gathering for breakfast. Suddenly, I heard Bob calling, "Jodi! Jodi!" "What?" I asked. He sounded horribly distressed! "Jodi, come here!" I thought for sure he was having a heart attack! I wasn't going to be able to go on the tour because God didn't want me to! I was resigned as I entered the room! Bob was sitting up! "You have to listen!" he said. "God has given me a song. You have to sing it… Oh, dear Lord!" As he began to sing the song, I realized God had indeed answered the questions in both of our minds! Never again did we question whether I was called to go out, or that he was called to the sacrifice of loneliness or financial burden… **Cost Of A Soul** was imprinted on Bob's heart and mind that morning and has been his mantra for ministry ever since!

What is the cost, what is the cost,
What is the cost of a soul?
God gave His Son, Jesus on the cross was hung,
Oh, oh that is the cost of a soul.

God sent His Son out of heaven above,
That whoever believed would be won.
God gave His Son, that man would be won,
Come on now, that is the cost of a soul.

Jesus said I am the Way, the Truth, and the Life, just follow me today
Then He gave up His life on the cross for you and me
Oh, oh, that is the cost of a soul.

What is the cost, what is the cost,
What is the cost of a soul?
God gave His Son, Jesus on the cross was hung,
Oh, oh what will you do for a soul?

What will you do? What will you give?
That whomever you know, they might live

What can you give, that they might live
Come on now, THAT is the cost of a soul!

I left feeling Bob's blessing and the Lord's confirmation. Some of my voice students joined me for a few events as well! It was a wonderfully successful tour in so many ways, but most importantly, I knew deep down at the end of each day, God was saying, "Well done, my good and faithful servant."

I Am A Survivor!
Wonderful opportunities realized and friendships made! J<><

Cecile Corbiere was a foster mom who had begun voice lessons with me in support of her foster daughter. She had become a wonderful friend to me. As traveling companions, we two girls headed out together. Cecile's brother, Rob Poirier, came out of the crowd after our concert in Yorkton and said, "I feel that God is showing me I'm supposed to create a website for you!" What a blessing! So many good things came out of my long-term partnership with Rob!

My life experiences are not always easily understood, but those who also want "more" of all the Lord has for them easily embrace the lessons I have learned! I see how God took me on that tour to build awareness of a charitable foundation and the touring life which I was called to. Some of the lessons were really difficult. Monies promised but not received; personality conflicts among ministry team members, etc. God knitted my heart together with many of the people I met on that road.

Bob found God faithful, too. He blessed the tour with expenses paid from offerings and CD sales. The pre-release of **Second Chance**, was literally hot off the press and placed in my hand at Caronport as I traveled from Swift Current to Moose Jaw the first week. Most importantly, God showed me that His ways are not our ways, but they are always right!

From Prince Albert (PA) to Yorkton on the final day of the tour, I was stopped by a police officer for speeding! Financially, I was just barely covering my expenses and couldn't believe my bad luck! I was also on a real thin timeline to get from the service Juanita and I had just celebrated in PA to Yorkton, in time for the Sunday evening concert to help kick off the CGMA convention. God allowed the police officer to be gracious and forgiving and *not* give me a ticket! He did say there would be at least two or three more cops between where I was and my destination so I might as well accept the fact that I would be late!

Arriving in Yorkton, I felt so unsure of myself. I didn't know these people, even though they seemed to know me. It turned out the format of the concert was similar to that of the traditional "Gaither Homecoming Sing-A-Longs", where the special guests all sat on stage in a half circle. Each of the artists took a turn standing up and singing a song. It was a heartwarming and welcoming way to begin what would be a life-changing event.

An amazing thing happened during that week! I felt that I had finally come home. Here I was in the middle of a bunch of people who totally loved Jesus and it wasn't all about the performance. It was all about a call that was on our lives to be obedient and do what we were supposed to be doing! This is where I became grounded and figured out who I was going to be as an artist. Each morning began with a meditative Loving the Lord session (worshiping from a heart of gratitude). Afternoon sessions were very timely too as veteran music ministers explained how they'd learned to survive being on the road, asking for bookings, etc. Through the evening "sing and share" sessions, each of the artists attending had the opportunity to sing, but additionally and probably more importantly, we were also invited to share from our hearts, why we were singing the chosen song.

At the end of that week, I received five awards: Female Vocalist of the Year, Female Entertainer of the Year, Reciter of the Year, Lyricist of the Year and New Artist of the Year. So, in 2005, my career as an award winning vocalist began! Credibility was now mine! The awards were definite proof of my second chance! My gift was recognized and through the years, both Bob and I have received many awards from the Country Gospel Music Association as well as other accolades. This was all in spite of the fact that I never wanted to be a country singer! LOL!

Interestingly enough, the local public television company recorded the opening concert and the nominee nights. This enhanced my exposure. After my first set of awards, I began to do radio and newspaper interviews, sharing my testimony and the reasons for the hope I'd found in Jesus. Bookings became easier to secure and my schedule on the road grew!

Driving long distances to perform over weekends, then getting back home for students or to be with Bob, was proving to be financially unviable. Paying my band mates for their work often left Bob and me 'in the red', so we prayed about how this new ministry life was to unfold.

On July 1st, 2006 Bob retired from his thirty-two years in education and joined me on the road. A new laptop held all my sound tracks so we were free to travel without a band. I'll admit now it was absolutely brutal at times! Difficult....and yet fulfilling! God told me we were to claim the nation for Jesus. We traveled as many as 325 days a year on the highways and byways... from east to west coast across Canada! To Branson and Nashville – from concert halls to prisons and parking lots to seniors' homes!

Discovering how God 'connects the dots' is pretty cool! J<><

We owned the house in Medicine Hat that we'd taken in on trade before the move to Saskatchewan. Even though I felt we should own a rental property, Bob really wasn't too enthusiastic about it. He had owned rental property before and felt that it was way too much work. But really, things had turned out well as the house became a place of true sanctuary for my girlfriends and their children. Now, a few years later, they were ready to move on. They gave notice that they would be departing.

It was at this time that I was at a women's event for a pregnancy shelter. I had been to several events over the years and felt committed to help them raise awareness to build a shelter for unwed moms. I thought it strange that I felt such an incredible burden for unwed moms and didn't understand why this burden was upon me. During the event that night, the Holy Spirit spoke to me, telling me that I was supposed to give my rental house to the project.

My immediate response was, "Oh no! Bob is going to kill me!"

Up to this point we had been receiving rent and our expenses were being covered. However, I knew beyond a shadow of a doubt that I was supposed to make this offer to the proposed shelter group.

I heard the Holy Spirit say, "Tell Maria that you are going to give her your house." While my first instinct was to say I would pray about it for a while, I must interject, "That is something we as Christians so often do when we hear God asking us to do something. We say that we will pray about it. No! No! Just do it! If you hear it, if you sense it, just go do it!"

Full of trepidation, I walked up to Maria and told her that the Holy Spirit had asked me to give this house to her. Maria got all teary-eyed and replied, "The Holy Spirit told me today that someone was going to give me a house."

Since Maria already had this idea planted in her heart earlier in the day, she had a plan. They would accept the *use* of the house though they wouldn't be able to pay rent (which I was totally okay with). They would, however, cover all the expenses such as utilities and taxes. They would also maintain it, make improvements and leave it even better. The transaction was solidified so quickly that it was almost unbelievable. Later that night, I phoned my girlfriend and took Maria over to view the house.

Problems began happening at the board level within the organization and there was great dissension among the ranks. There was even a rumor that they didn't want to deal with me because I had been in and out of mental institutions all of my life. For her own peace of mind, Maria phoned me to inquire about the rumors. I was shocked and laughed a bit saying, "Well, no, not me! My ex-husband has been in and out of Five North a little bit. I don't know for sure where this is coming from." It was really awful to learn of the word curses that had been spoken over me and my life by people who were known to this group. There were other things that happened. The owners of a bar in town had heard about this pregnancy shelter and offered them $25,000 to get the house and running, but the Board of Directors declined the offer since they felt the money was coming from 'heathens'.

Maria and I prevailed and went ahead with things. House parents were chosen and anointed for the ministry and they set up housekeeping. It was some time later that I was invited to meet the first baby that was born there and to see the home they had created. They had done so much with the house! It was updated with paint and faux marble finishes here and there. I was overwhelmed with how they had totally changed the house.

As I sat there, I was still somewhat curious, wondering and pondering it all! I still didn't get why I had felt called to partner with them. I had done it totally out of obedience. I even verbalized these words to the housemother saying it was curious because I still didn't really have a heart for unwed moms, and didn't really understand why God would ask me to do this. The housemother told me she knew exactly why this happened. She asked that we just remain quiet for a minute. (I could joke that people may wonder how I could remain quiet at all! LOL!) She asked that we pray and said, "Father God, I know that you want Jodi to know why partnering in this project was important for her. So we are just going to quietly sit and wait for you to show her why she needed to be part of this project."

We quieted our hearts and minds and sat there. No more than about three minutes elapsed when tears started rising up out of my innermost being. I said, "If I hadn't been born, maybe my grandma would have loved my mom more!" I didn't know that I had ever felt this way. It had never been evident to me before. Almost as if I was speaking from my mother's womb, I hear myself say, "I was conceived out of wedlock. I sense a spirit of disqualification on me. I believe I'm a mistake!" At this moment, I began to unpack all the lies that I had received right in the womb; that I was not valuable and that, if I'd been conceived in today's generation, I might have been aborted. It blew me away to discover the ways the enemy had me believing such horrible untruths. My parents married just months after I was conceived, raised me and gave me a wonderful, loving home. My eyes were opened to the reasons why I had always struggled with feelings of insecurity and low self-esteem. This all started another deeply moving and truly healing journey for me. In fact, the housemother and her partner in ministry began to meet with me regularly for inner healing counseling. This helped me discover all the lies I had believed within myself since conception. We took each issue that would arise and replaced those lies with the truth of God's love for me.

When I was asked if I'd known prior to this experience that I was conceived before my parents were married, I said I had made the discovery when I was about twelve years old. Isn't it amazing that just because I was obedient to give the house to them, I would be allowed to experience restoration that continued to grow? Really cool! LOL!

The pregnancy shelter story is very important in my life. I fully believe it was so that I could move into a place of greater peace. Sadly, due to the struggles within the organization, the project did not turn out to be as financially viable as it needed to be. After a couple of years they decided they had to shut down.

The rental house would become a bit of a challenge for Bob and me, although we were undecided about whether to sell the house or not. We began to feel the 'season' of being landlords might be coming to an end!

OH, THAT YOU WOULD BLESS ME INDEED
AND ENLARGE MY TERRITORY J<><

One day while I was in Calgary for a music conference, I went to a music store with a friend. As we were standing in line waiting to pick up an order that had arrived, I thought I would just wander around and see what they had in the store for Gospel music. There was a sense of oppression that I felt upon entering the store and it seemed like a dark place. I told the Lord it didn't feel like a great place to be. This may have been part of the curiosity to see what they had for Gospel music.

In this huge national retailer of music, HMV, there was a whole row probably about three to five feet running from top to bottom. The Gospel row was completely empty, except on the very bottom where there was one CD by Bob Dylan (who is actually a Messianic Jew). There was not another single Christian artist being represented in the whole store. That means quite possibly there was not any other Christian representation in the whole HMV music chain across Canada.

Standing in front of that empty rack, I spoke out loud, "In Jesus' name, I claim this space for my music and for people like me, who share our stories of how we found hope in Jesus. And in Jesus' name, I am going to believe that my music is going to be in HMV, and that people like me are going to be given the opportunity to distribute in this place." After my friend finished purchasing her CD, we left.

The whole experience haunted me over the remainder of the day and into the night. It really bothered me that it was not possible to walk into this music store and purchase any type of Gospel music. If regular people off the street were actually seeking the Lord, where would they be able to get Gospel music?

That year I had registered for the Covenant Award Weekend, which is the equivalent of the U.S. 'Dove' Awards. In conjunction with the awards, the Canadian Gospel Music Association (GMA) hosted their big convention in Calgary each year and I was going to be there.

My first album, **Second Chance**, had been nominated for Country Gospel Album of the Year a few years before. Bob's song, **Book of Life**, had also been nominated as Children's Song of the Year. These were some of the interesting confirmations that we had received that we were supposed to be involved in country gospel music even though we had not previously realized it. This helped to encourage us and spur us on and in a sense, send us out.

The GMA does a great job recruiting good speakers and all types of industry people. They come with wisdom and experience specific to the Christian music industry. Representatives from a huge Christian music distributor attended, obviously looking for new recording artists. I enjoyed a conversation with one of their reps about the possibly of distributing my 'almost ready for distribution' newest album, **Now Is The Time.** According to him, I was not considered a regional artist, but rather a national artist. Bob and I had already traveled across Canada from Newfoundland to British Columbia. I could claim to have fans in every province, except maybe for Quebec. (I so can't speak French! I had given our tour bus driver a free CD though! LOL!) I was amazed that these music industry people were actually speaking to me with great respect because I had been across Canada and had a fan base across the country.

I went into a workshop that was presented by a couple of people in radio and media. A fellow spoke about a whole new strategy by Universal Music in Canada. They were looking to expose more gospel music throughout the country. My heart totally leapt at this idea! They discussed a distribution project where the artist would have to pay for the CDs up front. Universal would then get them pressed, manufactured and shipped to the warehouse. From there, Universal Music would have them listed in their catalogue and any music store would have access to ordering them. Therefore, anybody could walk into a store and ask for a specific CD or music by a particular artist and would be able to buy it. (People would now be able to go into the store and ask for a Jodi Faith CD because I had been in their area and they had heard me sing.)

After considerable discussion with this man after his session, I was very intrigued and he was very gracious. He was excited about who I was and what my music might offer. I told him, "I'm no teenage, 'b-boppin' music girl here! This is a country gospel album that I am getting ready to release." However, the guy still wanted to have a listen to it, so I gave it to him. The next day he started talking to me about the distribution deal. I was questioning him and was unsure of the situation, considering all the people that were there. He told me, "There is one group in all of Canada right now targeting this market, and it is the Gaithers. The only people selling music on a national level are the Gaithers and the Gaither Vocal Band. The music you've recorded and are going to sell will target that same audience (demographic forty to seventy year-olds). This is exactly the type of music we are looking to cover."

At the time, I was staying at my daughter's place and again, I hardly slept a wink that night. I kept thinking about whether I should phone him and suggest he consider coming to hear me sing. It was astounding that this guy was planning to distribute my music and he had never even heard me sing live. He didn't really know the whole package and was simply basing everything on this album that he had listened to.

I went to the awards ceremony the next evening. In my anxiety I asked God for a sign that this was actually supposed to happen. I was on my way to the ladies' room and who was standing there, but this Don Summerville fellow that I had been chatting with, the actual A & R representative for Universal Music Company.

I was a bit astounded and told him, "I didn't know if I should call you and I'm just not sure what to make of all this."

Don responded, "Well, what is to make of it?"

My reply was, "Why would you pursue an unknown artist like me?"

"First of all, you are not unknown. You have had national exposure. You have already sold a couple thousand CDs. But most of all, I think we can sell the package, the Jodi Faith package!" was Don's answer.

I inquired, "Why would I deal with you instead of the Christian music distributor who is offering me some sort of deal over there? He looked me straight in the eye and here is what he said. "Because! I've been listening to you talk for the last couple of days. And from what I hear, you have a missionary heart. You are not really interested in singing for the 'found', but you want to sing for the 'lost'. Jodi, I can put your music in HMV and Wal-Mart across Canada."

Remember that I had been standing in an HMV store claiming that space for mine and other's music! I was absolutely rocked! After all, this man didn't know the story of me being in the store at all. The only person who could have known was God Himself. I felt deep within my spirit that I needed to do this. I also thought it was ironical and perhaps prophetic that I was being offered a distribution deal with Universal Music, when I had committed to producing the album with Wes Bloom of Universal Sound Studios in Assiniboia, SK. I remember how God had shown me He 'was taking me to the nations' when we had begun discussing the purchase of a home in Arizona!

"Ok, then! LOL!" I thought! "Wow, Lord!" I prayed, "take me to the universe! I'm ready!" LOL! We continued discussing the new album. I had the artwork underway. Some of the tracks had been done and had just arrived back from Virginia. It was sounding pretty good. I committed to some serious work in studio with Wes, while Don said he'd discuss my pending deal with his bosses and get back to me as soon as possible.

I headed home to Bob who wasn't with me the whole weekend and had not heard any of the conversations between myself and Don.

I told Bob, "Yeah, I've been offered this distribution deal with Universal Music."

Bob said, "Oh great!" He was not very enthused because all he could see were growing expenses!

We argued back and forth a bit. I explained that the HMV 'sign' was all the confirmation I needed.

Bob asked the usual question, "Well, how are you going to pay for it?"

"I don't know what the deal is yet. Don is going to send me the contract and we're going to look at it. I am just going to have to believe that if it is meant to be, whatever money I need, *will* be in the bank at that moment."

Bob made it clear that he would not give me any money for the distribution deal. I would have to come up with it on my own. I was okay with this arrangement. Most recording artists that I met up to this time had to take out bank loans to do anything with their music. If you were going to publish a book or record a song, you pretty much had to take out a loan. It was in the back of my mind that I might be eligible for a loan.

Reconnecting with the past for ministry opportunities in the future! J<><

After the conference, Bob and I traveled to sing at a little church in Pincher Creek, AB where I was doing a ladies' event. At the end of the night, a woman walked up to me and introduced herself as someone who had gone to church with my family years before.

She said, "You're Jodi Heidebrecht."

To which I replied, "Yeah."

She explained how she and her husband along with my parents had been youth leaders together. She said she'd loved to hear me in church sing as a little girl. She couldn't believe that she had just heard my story of how I had been forbidden to sing for seventeen years in my marriage. It blew her away! We had such an amazing visit together. Bob and I enjoyed lunch the next day with her and her husband. It was such a neat experience since I felt it was reminiscent of the Full Circle Tour and it just brought everything together so nicely. God was taking me back, connecting me to my old congregation and the church family that I had been part of until I was sixteen. I vaguely remembered these people as they shared experiences from years before. Bob and I learned much about them and their lives since that time. They then asked whether I would consider coming to do a Christmas concert for them. That was exciting to me as I'd be able to keep in touch with this couple I had just reconnected with. It was cool how one concert would turn into a second opportunity for ministry.

In the meantime, I received my contract from Universal Music stating I would have to provide a cheque for $5,300.00 on the day we were to meet and sign the contract in Calgary. This was a neat part of the story too, as I had been praying for a way to be able to spend more time in Alberta and be near my children, especially my daughter in Airdrie. My prayer had been that God would open up my calendar so that instead of being on the other side of the country, I could be in Alberta. It was super exciting as I read the contract and realized I was required to attend meeting in Calgary, right next to where my daughter lived. The main question now was how I was going to raise $5,300 when all I had in my bank account at the time was about $300. LOL! I knew Bob wasn't going to give me any money and this was only the beginning of the process. The deal would also require me to come up with another $15,000 to buy/supply the first 5,000 CDs when it was ready for production. I wasn't going to panic though, because I believed I had received the sign from God as Don had spoken with me. I knew that everything would work out. It was a feeling of knowing it was going to be just fine.

A month and half later I went back to Pincher Creek with the awesome news that I had the opportunity for a recording deal with Universal Music and that I had to raise $5,000 to make it happen. I shared the story, and my joy about the fact that God obviously wanted my music to be available in the market place and how excited I was about that fact.

Upon getting back home from the Christmas tour, I set out to do a yearend newsletter. Bob's and my ministry was operating through The Great Commission Foundation (GCF) at the time, so if people wanted a tax receipt for donations they could give through this Foundation. One day I spoke with Jo-Ellen (the secretary at the GCF) and explained that I was going to be doing a sponsorship blitz as I needed to raise money for this CD distribution deal. I wanted her opinion and together we created a letter. Bob and I stuffed mailboxes and approached our many supporters.

Jo-Ellen phoned the last week of December and said, "Usually all gifts remain anonymous, but I have to tell you what just happened." At this point, it was only two weeks from when the contract was supposed to be signed in Calgary. And it was nearing the end of the year for charitable giving tax receipts to be issued.

"We just received a $5,000 donation for your CD distribution project!" she said! I was overcome and just started bawling my eyes out. By this time I had less than $300 in my account. Jo-Ellen asked if it would be all right to call the people and ask them about revealing their identity Usually, the donations come in and the Foundation writes a letter on our behalf thanking the donor for the gift. In this situation she said, she felt like I should know who the people were that had been so generous. She felt it would really encourage Bob and me. I agreed. I really wanted to be able to thank them personally. It was so hard for me to imagine anyone giving such a large sum of money.

A short time later Jo-Ellen phoned after contacting the couple. With their permission we discovered it was the couple we'd had lunch with in Pincher Creek. Folks who had known me as a child, who had gone to church with my family and had believed so much in the gift God had given me. They had been so moved by my story and how God had been rebuilding my life. After seventeen years of my not singing, they considered it a wonderful blessing to sow into this project. For Bob who is often skeptical about things like this, there was no question that when I received exactly the amount of money I needed to have in my bank account it proved this to be from God. The money was there!

I'm a Lady of Destiny, living my fantasies, Living abundantly! Thank God I'm ME!! J<><

Off to Calgary I went to sign the contract. As I drove down the road I had a conversation with God. After all, their side of the deal promised that D2 Records/IKON/Universal would put advertising on radio stations all across Canada in order for people to know I was touring and that the new Jodi Faith album was available for purchase. There would be radio advertising and media with promotions attached to it. I'd had a quick visit with my family, my daughter-in-law and grandchildren in Medicine Hat. I drove along singing and praying and just being excited about going to be where my daughter was and staying with her. Everything was just perfect! Although Bob wasn't with me we were on the same page, too! Life was so good! LOL!

As I was singing and thinking, I told the Lord that if I was going to have this deal, I should really have a jingle. It should summarize my life story. I actually laughed out loud at the whole thought of it. I thought it should be some kind of a crossover song with an obvious country gospel sound. It had to be something that any woman could relate to. How would I tell my story in a song? A tune started coming to me and suddenly, the *Lady of Destiny* song was born!

> *I am proof that dreams come true and you can have it all*
> *Ain't no need to stand there with your back against the wall*
> *A journey of a thousand miles, starts with that first step*
> *And darlin' long as you have breath you're not finished yet!!*

I'm a lady of destiny, livin' my fantasies,
Livin' abundantly… hey there, come join me!
Footloose and fancy free, livin' God's plans for me
A lady of destiny, thank God I'm Me!

I'm driving and writing at the same time! I've placed those itty-bitty post-it notes I am using all over the dash, my mirror and the front seat.…I am totally hyper! I'm amazed at the download I'm getting! The song is amazing! As the second stanza comes and flows.… I am feeling fantastic and just giggling to myself. LOL!

I used to lay in bed and hide my head and cry and sigh and pray
Couldn't stand the thought of living through one more lousy day
Then I stood on up, said enough's enough I was ready for a change!
Took my life back by the horns – giving destiny the reins!

I'm a lady of destiny, livin' my fantasies,
Livin' abundantly… hey there, come join me!
Footloose and fancy free, livin' God's plans for me
A lady of destiny, thank God I'm free!

I was now nearing Bassano and only about an hour from Calgary. I needed to change for my meeting so I stopped at a truck stop. A coffee was definitely needed, so I poured myself a cup of decaf, but it was cold. That was unbelievable! I really needed a coffee because it often calms me down a bit. A lady was working so I asked if I would be able to bother her for a fresh cup of decaf coffee. The lady was very apologetic and I assured her it wasn't a big deal. In an excited manner, I told her how I had just written a jingle for a distribution deal across Canada. Hyper, I said, "I just believe that God loves you so much that I am supposed to sing it for you! I don't know. Would you like to listen to it? Do you believe in God?" I asked her.

"Well, I *am* the pastor's wife at the little Evangelical Free Church here." I felt there couldn't be anyone better to hear it. I ran out to my car and grabbed all my little post-it notes and put them in order and began to sing. As I sang, the lady got these huge tears and said, "It's amazing!" I said, "Really?" I was totally reassured by her response. The coffee was brewed and I was on my way. We offered each other a word of blessing as I went.

It wasn't until that moment that I realized that women were going to be moved to tears by the truth of this amazing song. I told God how awesome He was and then bawled all the way to Calgary. I kept practicing the song and have never changed a word.

In Calgary, I walked into the restaurant knowing full well that I could pay the $5,333.33 because I had it! I walked up to Don Summerville and said, "I just wrote a jingle and I think it needs to be on the album." We were meeting to sign a contract on the album that was already finished. Don had heard it and had already agreed that the album was complete. Now, out of the blue, I was throwing this at him! He told me that it could possibly be added.

In the middle of the restaurant was a table of about six or eight women having lunch. I got up and approached them. I said, "Hi, I'm Jodi Faith. Sorry to bother you, but I'm here signing a contract for a distribution deal for my new CD with my A & R guy who is Don Summerville. I just wrote a song today and I need to know whether or not it should be on the album. Would you be willing to listen to me sing this song for you?"

The women were sitting there looking at me like I was something from another planet. One lady spoke up and said they would gladly listen and then all vote for or against. So once again I sang the song from my little post-it notes. These ladies jumped to their feet and were hooting and clapping and yelling, "Yes! I want a destiny!" "I love that song!" "When is it going to be available?" and "I want to buy it!" LOL!

Don agreed to meet me later that evening with the voice recorder. He became the percussion providing rhythm while I sang my song. I still have the copy of me singing it for the first time on Don's voice recorder without any music. *Lady of Destiny* arrived in Nashville and some of the most amazing artists added their talents to the project! Our studio guy did up the track within a couple of weeks. He brought the song back up to Canada and I traveled to Calgary to add vocals in Don's studio. *Lady Of Destiny* ended up being the first song on the **Now Is The Time** album and distribution plans evolved quickly! Now I just had to believe when the time came, I *would* have the additional $15,000 required to manufacture the first five thousand albums.

WE NEED A SIGN!! AGAIN, GOD, I KNOW YOUR WAYS ARE
NOT OUR WAYS
SO I'VE GOTTA ASK YOU TO SHOW US WHAT TO DO! J<><

As one renter came and went from my rental property in Medicine Hat, another lady with a grown daughter, who was trying to get over a 'meth' addiction, moved in. Even my compassion started to wane, as the rent wasn't paid. When we discovered that the tenants had moved out under cover of darkness, we knew we were done!

Mysteriously perhaps, at the same time these people moved out, I was struggling with God about Bob's desire to move to Arizona (AZ). I did again, what I had become so good at doing; I put out a fleece. Bob had been playing baseball in AZ and loved the Phoenix area. He *had* told me before we were ever married that he intended to live in the south, enjoy the major league baseball spring training and escape the Canadian winters! But was it really God's plan? I had a difficult time with the idea of being there because I felt I was called as a missionary to Canada. When we first discussed the possibility, it just didn't seem possible that God would be alright with our going to Arizona, but I know God began showing me it was His will for us to go. Bottom line was: Shut up and honor your husband! LOL! I sensed God saying, Bob wants to go to Arizona so you need to go to Arizona. I started to process how to honor my husband. I began praying! "God, we will only be there for March so if it's your will for us to live there eventually, You will have to sell my rental house. It'll have to happen quickly though, Lord, and we will need a guaranteed deal so that we'll know how much money we can spend on a vacation home."

Sure enough, we listed the house, left for AZ and on the 10th of March we had an offer. The following day our realtor and good friend phoned and told us we had another offer? This would mean the first people would have to remove all their conditions and would have to go to their bank and get a letter stating they definitely had the financing secured and money available on the closing date.. There would be no way they could back out of the deal and Bob and I would get the exact amount of money we needed to go house hunting in Arizona. Before we left Arizona that March, we had a house selected down there. It was located in Venture Out, a resort community of 1749 park models, (never to be called trailers)! It was 925 sq. ft. including the addition which we learned was called an "Arizona room." It was really cool how God was showing me that it was okay with Him for us to live in Arizona! He showed me how it was going to work, too!

Bob and I actually believe God created another miracle in the whole scenario! The seller of the home in AZ had been diagnosed with what seemed to be terminal kidney failure. These folks thought they would not be returning. Bob and I told them that if they were in any shape to be able to do so, they could rent the house back from us. The gentleman experienced great healing and God opened the door for them to return and they rented the house from us for the first couple of years.

An amazing part of the story is also how the market values had increased since I had first purchased the home. God grew the equity in the house so that by the time I had to write my next cheque for the total value of the CD distribution package, the house was sold and the money was in the bank! There was equity in the amount of exactly $15,000 left over to pay for the manufacture of those albums, and just in time to meet the deadline! LOL!

I had been thinking that one day we might return and settle in Medicine Hat, but I let go of all those plans for our future in order to live in the fullness of God's plans at that moment! Definitely a powerful lesson learned!

RELIGION THAT GOD OUR FATHER ACCEPTS AS PURE AND FAULTLESS IS THIS TO LOOK AFTER ORPHANS AND WIDOWS IN THEIR DISTRESS. JAMES 1:27 (NIV) J<><

The house in Arizona was purchased, paperwork signed, and Bob and I returned to Canada with a new sense of direction. Arriving home that spring, I felt I'd entered a new season. A shift had definitely taken place. I felt that I was on the cusp of accelerated growth and had a deep sense that I was supposed to fast! I had never actually fasted before and had never heard anyone teach on fasting either, but felt I should do so. Deep down, I realized that I was worried that I'd use the fast as a way to lose weight! I continued to pray and wait for the Lord's guidance.

Now having the contract signed with Universal, I was obligated to get my music out there and promote my music internationally. Don, my A&R guy, helped me understand this would create "buzz" about me and my music. I paid a radio tracker to send my music out across Canada, while at the same time I sent my music to New Christian Music in the UK. Almost immediately, reports of my songs flying up the chart overseas were received. My **Lady of Destiny** song was at #1 for sixteen weeks, while my version of Russ Scherer's song ***Random Acts of Kindness*** was at #1 for thirty-two weeks! Russ wept at the news his song was being so-o-o well received!

Say good morning to your neighbor.
Give your enemy a smile.
Do random acts of kindness, go the extra mile.
Do good to those who hurt you.

Yes, start with that good deed.
By doing so you'll plant a better seed.

I had to laugh out loud again as I watched how God was using His country music gifts in me to reach the world! And to think I'd fought singing country for so long! LOL!

While my radio tracker was watching my songs doing so well internationally, radio airplay was a lot tougher for me in Canada. My success overseas opened doors and I received an invitation to attend the Hank Snow Country Music Tribute Weekend in Bridgewater, Nova Scotia that August! I agreed to attend although no expenses would be paid. I was booked to sing in the Gospel Music Showcase and would also present in the Songwriter's Circle. While booking my flight and praying for CD sales, I suddenly had the inspiration to connect with the Bridgewater Red Hat group. As a regular entertainer for them in the west, I was welcomed. They would even host a concert for me, which would help with expenses! The greatest blessing was the way the Queen of the local chapter said I could stay with them for no charge! Their lovely home was just a few blocks from the venue! What a gift my connection to her and my Red Hat sisters was!

As Bob and I continued traveling and singing across western Canada, it seemed more doors opened because of the Universal deal. I met the Pinel Family that spring and invited them to tour with us. Singing and dancing together, the "mom and three daughter team" were just awesome and the audiences absolutely loved them. Every time they danced, I was moved to tears. The week of performing during Calgary Stampede was especially challenging! Amid 30+ Celsius temperatures, there was lots of running through big city traffic from corporate BBQ's and customer/staff appreciation days to ministering at soup kitchens and Stampede breakfasts! After ten days I was exhausted! It was Sunday morning and I had just presented the Stampede Queen and Princesses with commemorative Bibles at the Alberta Christian Cattlemen's Breakfast. I remember asking God if He could just please make a way for me to find an air-conditioned church; a place of rest where I could just escape by myself for a time of respite. Bob had gone to play ball with his friends in Red Deer and the dance team had left for Saskatoon. Almost miraculously, I was able to find a church very near my exit from the Stampede Park. Although I'd never be able to find it again, my time there that day would change my life forever.

The welcome was warm and the air cool. The spirit of the Lord was sweet as I closed my eyes and simply rested. As the worship music was presented, I truly felt my weary soul being restored. I was actually moved to tears; it was such a relief. Then the preacher got up and in his thundering voice said, "So! What have you done for a widow or an orphan lately?" I tried to ignore him, but he repeated himself again loudly! I remember indignation rising up in me as I thought, "Are you kidding me? I have been running, working, ministering all week here, Lord! In the highways and byways… soup kitchens and parking lots… Could someone else please help the widows? Please!" Well, by the time he'd finished his sermon, I was willing to admit I was very wrong. The pastor had presented a strong argument and I repented. "Please, show me a widow, Lord, and I'll help her! I promise!"

Just a month later, I was in Bridgewater for the Hank Snow weekend! My hosts were amazing as they had filled their fridge and invited me to please make lunches so I could keep my expenses to a minimum! After a great festival weekend I asked my hosts if I could take them out for dinner. "Maybe there is somewhere you'd like to go, but haven't been?" I asked. A few restaurants were named, but only one would be open the Sunday evening we had free. Cranberry's had just opened in the newly restored historic Fairview Inn. My hosts were excited to see what restorations had been done and our server offered a tour of the place after our exceptional meal!

As we followed our tour guide, we learned a Canadian couple had purchased the Inn after returning from Sri Lanka. Pamela and Gerry Porodo had started a humanitarian aid foundation, helping the survivors of the tsunami rebuild their lives. Suddenly my friends and I were standing in the middle of the parlor surrounded by hundreds of pieces of jewelry and handbags. Work For Widows tags were attached to each piece that included a photo of a woman who had beaded the item and her personalized empowerment statement. "By purchasing this item you help me rebuild my life after my husband died."…. "By being in this program my children and I have hope for our future!"…. "I can buy medicine that will help me live."

I remembered my pledge from just one month before! I'd said I would help the widows and orphans and knew I needed to help this cause. A remarkable thing was that Pamela was available, on site instead of in Sri Lanka and we were able to set a meeting time. I returned the next morning to discuss how to help. My heart was moved by the stories Pamela told me of the women they were helping through the foundation. Pam checked out my website and listened to my songs on the Internet and said these could be the widows' songs! I left Bridgewater with a suitcase full of jewelry and as an ambassador for the new program Pam and I had just created. Please see www.workforwidows.com.

My music was being played all over the world. I was becoming known as their "International Ambassador" and during each event we'd share the Work For Widows development program and sell their amazing jewelry! Suddenly the songs I sang were shared as proof that just as I had overcome the storms of life, the widows could, too!

Today, I am known as a total crossover artist. Songs from the **Now Is The Time** album were being distributed and played on radio in Europe and overseas to 50+ nations. I received notice one day that I'd been named the Middle of the Road Artist of the Year for the New Christian Music (NCM) Distribution Group in the UK. At first I felt that didn't sound all that flattering until I asked exactly what that meant. Most contemporary worship stations, as well as most country gospel stations had voted for me! Wow! God was taking my talent and using me in a myriad of places. Charlotte would say, I'd hit the perfect place, loved and appreciated by both country and contemporary genres! Truly though, having been obedient to walk through the doors the Lord had opened I was blessed beyond words to say the least!

PROPHETIC WORDS PROPEL US FORWARD,
CONFIRM THE VISIONS AND DREAMS INSIDE
US AND INSPIRE US TO BELIEVE FOR THE
FUTURE GOD HAS PLANNED FOR US! J<><

At a retreat, the Full Gospel Couples Advance, a mentor and friend approached me one morning after our session together. She said she had 'watched the mantle of prophetic worship coming down out of the heavens to fall on my shoulders'. As she spoke over me, I began to feel a warm anointing surround me, confirmation flowing all over me. As tears filled my eyes, I said "Thank you. Thank you, Lord!"

As we went our own ways to have lunch, a spirit of confusion and anxiety began to fall on me almost immediately. I realized I had no clue what her words meant! LOL! Embarrassed, I shyly went back to my friend and said, "I haven't a clue what prophetic worship is!" My mentor explained it as 'creative song that just flows out of you'! Oh! I could understand that! LOL! I said that happened to me all the time as I was engaged in corporate worship – songs just rising up in me! Songs I'd sing 'over' the songs being sung! "Exactly!" my friend said! "In fact, the best prophetic worshipper I know is Joanne McFatter! If you get a chance, go onto the Internet and Google her. That will help you understand the gift God has given you today!"

After lunch, Bob and I went up to our room. Almost immediately he fell asleep, but I was too excited to settle wondering about this new thing God was going to do with me. Restless, I finally got up and went to the computer. A most beautiful website opened up before me as I searched for more info on Joanne McFatter. Ethereal... delicate... beautiful... soothing... *until* I began to read. It appeared that Joanne was a quantum physicist or some scary thing! Anxiety hit me over the head! I'd barely passed math, never mind the science of... "Oh, God, oh, God, what are You doing?" My stomach flipped! I was literally feeling sick – there was NO WAY God could be calling me to *this*!

Stop! I felt the spirit of authority rising up in me! I could feel the word, STOP, rising up again! I began to pray in the spirit – saying there was no way Satan was going to steal this from me! Long story short, God showed up eventually and calmed my fears! "Oh my! Crazy, eh?" LOL!

I know now I *am* called to prophetic worship in an entirely new way, different from Joanne McFatter perhaps, but that's okay! The greatest desire of my heart is to minister as a worship leader. Engaged in a life as the solo artist and keynote speaker who sings, I usually follow the worship team instead of participating in it! I worship prophetically at home and have had a few opportunities to lead worship with AGLOW Women's Ministries. Most importantly, I will remain expectant. I have been faithful to all God has given me as I have traveled alone or with Bob. I'm excited about being given the opportunity to be the prophetic worshipper I am called to be... just as soon as He opens that door for me in a greater way!

A Royal Priesthood??
Here I am Lord, send me! J<><

We were attending the CGMA convention that June and experienced deep worship and intimacy with the Lord throughout the week. On the morning of the final worship session the Holy Spirit called me to fast! I started weeping and felt moved by the way God had dealt with me so gently and mercifully. He had definitely called me though, and although I could smell the most amazing lasagna meal baking in the fellowship hall, peace filled me as I prepared my heart to fast.

As we were leaving the worship session, our mentors and friends, Billy and Donna Hale, felt led to pray over the members as we left. As Bob and I stopped before them, a powerful word of prophecy was spoken over us saying "we were being elevated to a place of greater authority as King and Queen in the Kingdom of God!" They said," You had been found faithful and God is well pleased!" After leaving the prayer line, we felt somewhat rocked! We didn't have a clue what all this meant, but we said, "yes and amen" to whatever God had in store.

Sitting down to lunch, I was so-o-o blessed to be able to sit beside another friend. She and her husband had been pastors in the Pentecostal Assemblies of Canada for years. As we visited, I said I was fasting, but didn't have a clue what to do! My friend shared everything I needed to know!! I began a forty-day 'Daniel Fast' that day. I would eat fruit and vegetables only. Every time I felt hungry I'd pray in the spirit as instructed! I thought it was absolutely amazing how God took care of every little detail!

Just a week or so later, Bob and I went out for dinner. I had a most amazing veggie stir-fry! It was awesome and I felt guilty! As we left, I began talking to God! This fast was not the least bit difficult. "Lord" I said, "I need to do something deeper, I think? Something harder? Shouldn't this be more difficult?" I began praying. This fast was so important to me! I needed answers for our future! Upon arriving home, I Googled Daniel Fasts to see what I could do! Asking the Lord for clarity, direction and wisdom regarding where to serve and with whom, especially during these last days, I was seeking God's will for our lives. He was so faithful! Praying while searching the net, I was led directly to the End Time Handmaidens and Servants (ETH-S) Organization website. Not coincidentally I'm sure I learned their upcoming international convention was to be held in Manitoba at exactly the same time Bob and I were already booked in the Winnipeg area.

As I scrolled through their website, I began to read their requirements for membership and discovered their "fast!" "This one would be tough! Wowzers!" I thought. But I also knew that I needed to do it! Tears began to flow as I read the vows a new ETH-S member would take. Almost word for word some of these were the very words I had prayed in the spring of 1994 as I had rededicated my life to Jesus Christ! Lying on the floor in my parents' basement, crying out to God, I had dedicated every breath, every moment of my life to Him! No holds barred I'd prayed way back then, and now here in front of me were those same words! I was astounded! I had just prayed saying I wanted to go deeper and here it was before me! The most amazing thing was that their fast was twenty-one days. I had a full twenty-one days left to complete my fast and could begin the protocol as set before me. Boiling vegetables and drinking just the broth or drinking boiled water with a little honey and lemon in it and that was it! Each day as I fasted, I prayed the words of the vows I knew I would be taking in Winnipeg later that summer.

END-TIME HANDMAIDENS/SERVANTS VOWS

Lord, I give myself to You;
I give my life to You.
I want to be your End-Time Handmaiden/Servant;
I feel Your call;
I believe I was sent
To do the Will of my Father.
I will take orders from You.
I will submit to You.

I will let You break my will.
I will not seek for comfort
Nor high position,
Nor to do what I want to do.
Mine is the humblest task,
Or the most dangerous task;
By the grace of God I will do it.
I will sleep where You want me to sleep,
I will eat what You give me to eat,
And when I have nothing, I will not complain.
If I go to prison I will rejoice.
And I will praise You
Because You've been to prison for me.
I love You, Jesus;
I thank You for calling me,
And that You want me,
And that You can use me;
And all I can say is,
"Send the fire and burn up the sacrifice.
Fill me with Thy Holy Spirit
And give me a double portion of Thine anointing."
Amen

We registered for the convention that August strictly out of obedience, but honestly, with a sense of expectation. Oh, yes! It was an amazing conference! I was able to connect with my cousin, Martha Peters Stewart, who'd been a member for years! Deep down, I felt as though I'd come home! I was sad I hadn't been part of the organization before.

Arriving at the convention we were allowed to park our fifth wheel right in the hotel parking lot. We began meeting wonderful people immediately and felt so welcomed. The level of intimacy we experienced was startling. During a week of powerful teaching, while still seeking direction and deeply immersed in ministry and prayer, I began to feel the Holy Spirit pressing me with urgency to go to Israel. Some time before I had had a vision of myself in Israel – singing unto the Lord in prophetic worship – and I felt the Spirit saying over and over during this convention,

"Now Is The Time"... I discussed the possibilities with Bob and with his permission I approached Carol Morris, the national president of the Canadian ETH-S, asking about the possibility of a mission trip to Israel 'sooner rather than later'. Although Carol said she thought a trip would be unlikely before the next year, I still couldn't get over the sense of urgency I felt. I let it go and simply set out to 'wait upon the Lord'.

That same morning, after being invited to the stage to share my testimony and song, ETH-S Founder, Sister Gwen Shaw, spoke a powerful word over our ministry. In front of everyone gathered, she asked us to set up a booth and told the audience to buy my music and learn about our ministry! That same afternoon, I was at our newly set up booth becoming acquainted with two new convention friends from North Carolina. One of them, Mrs. Judy Ball of Breaker of Dawn Ministries, asked me to join them in intercession ministry to Israel during the Feast of Tabernacles hosted by the International Christian Embassy to Jerusalem. Although I was stunned by the automatic confirmation I felt, I was especially curious as to how it would evolve with less than two months to see it happen!

I had no doubt the Holy Spirit had opened this door and I was challenged by Judy to believe for provision in order to minister in Jerusalem that very season. The cost of the trip was $3500. Praying for the Lord's provision in order to walk through this new door was exciting.

Bob and I were ordained through the International Ministers Forum that week as well. As Sister Doris Schwartz and Sister Gwen prayed over us, we were slain in the Spirit and filled with a new boldness for evangelism and exhortation. We knew immediately that Sister Gwen would be an important mentor to us in the years to come. Paul Keith Davis spoke into my life during that week also. He asked whether others could see the glory on me as I sang. Another one of the speakers really spoke to the fact that we all needed to "ask for more!" She'd been a missionary in India with Sister Gwen and had written a book called, *Just One More Soul!* God had previously shown me that I needed to ask for more souls! I felt convicted and prayed also. Days later, the Lord showed me a number... it was huge! I could NOT even think about it without panicking! I laid the number at the feet of the Savior and said, "Whatever, however, you can do whatever you want with me, Lord, but I can't worry about it!" It was just way too scary!!

The money started to come in as we hosted a few concerts and sent out letters to our churches in the Hat (Hillcrest) and at Woodrow. Friends from Full Gospel in Calgary and area felt called to sow into the ministry trip also. One night when I was babysitting my grandsons, a friend called to say they wanted to bring me a cheque. She brought her young sons over for dinner and a visit. As we visited she said, "I feel that God wants you to go to Reinhard Bonnke tomorrow night!" I didn't know much about the minister and told my girlfriend I couldn't go as I'd offered to babysit the next night. Val reiterated the invitation, "Maybe something is up... maybe God wants you there?" As our visit came to an end and Val went to leave, she suddenly turned back to me and said, "I really feel God does *not* want me to leave without your promise that you come tomorrow night!" I promised, knowing the Holy Spirit was up to something. I said I'd bring my grandsons if I had to, but I would go!

The next evening I arrived at the hotel to see Mr. Bonnke. Up the stairs I went. As I came around the corner of the conference area I stopped in my tracks. Tears welled up in my eyes as I saw the banner that spanned the lobby. I read "100,000,000 Souls" – the exact number the Lord had impressed upon my heart weeks before. Much of what Mr. Bonnke said that night seemed to be just for me! Connections were made! Renewed friendships blossomed! I was in awe. Humbled and honored, I gave into the offering knowing the one hundred million souls I was called to minister to for the sake of the Kingdom might just be reached by partnering with his ministry! Like a farmer planting seed, I was sowing into their expected harvest and knew it was a great place to start regardless!

Israel was an amazing experience. With absolutely no way to make it happen on my own, God taught me an important lesson about submitting to His plans for my life and waiting on Him to do the miraculous! I am so very grateful for those who helped me financially and for those who also prayed. It was a remarkable trip! I was humbled by God's call on my life to go deeper in intercession, spiritual warfare, prayer and prophetic worship. I was blessed to minister with a team of amazing 'frontline warriors'. One of the team members had a vision of me one night. She said, "I see your breaker angel, Jodi! He is there, going ahead of you, breaking ground! You are called to new places and new things, but don't be afraid because your angel has gone ahead of you to make the way!" I was encouraged although everything was so new!

My heart was broken for Israel and I prayed that God would allow me to grow in my love of His chosen people! I found the spiritual oppression in Israel grieved my spirit deeply, but felt challenged daily to stay aligned with Christ, my eyes fully on Jesus – my only Master and King.

During the months after I returned home, ministry continued and we began planning things for our winter visit to Arizona. I was excited, working on how I was going to decorate the place, but I was still telling God that I didn't really understand it all. I did plan to decorate the office and en suite area with 'the globe', sensing God had literally taken us to the nations since this purchase! Words of prophesy spoken years before, had predicted this many times! The music was already going ahead of us.

Months later, having arrived in AZ, we were unpacking. I started going through boxes of stored items from my old Faith House home décor store. I'd decided we should simply haul all the leftover stock to AZ with the idea of repurposing and using as much of it as possible. As I opened the first of the dusty newspaper wrapped items, my mouth dropped open. In my hand was a "King!" The next item was the matching chalkware "Queen!" As I set them out to be spray-painted gold, I felt tears welling up in my eyes as the words spoken over us the summer before came back to me. "Oh, dear Lord, please help me understand all you have for us in this new land! In this new season! Help me always remember YOU brought us here for Your purposes and for exactly such a time as this!" Our home is full of reminders of the call on our lives to live as "a royal priesthood!"

What I hadn't realized is that Arizona is full of Canadians all over the place. It was God's witty way of having us meet more Canadians and make more friends. Going to church with them, singing in choir together, attending Bible studies and prayer groups and serving in outreach opportunities has been a huge blessing! We were meeting people from all across Canada and the States. These new friends were inviting us to come to their towns to sing, share and tell our stories. I hadn't realized how lonely life on the road had been either. Being part of a winter resort has allowed us to plug into community again; building relationships, visiting with people, playing ball and participating in community theatre!

I then realized that God had set us up to take the house on trade all those years earlier as a way of preparing us for our destiny to be fulfilled in Arizona. Being obedient to my husband proved to be God's way of blessing my life. Who knew? LOL!

"The prayers of the saints are before the Lord forever." (Revelation 8:4) J<><

God extended His grace to me in a very precious way in the summer of 2009. Through the years I was always able to share my deepest needs and fears with my Oma. When I had deep concerns about my children's lives, hurts or hang-ups, Oma and I would be able to pray together over them.

When Oma passed away in 2009 at the age of 93, I mourned intensely because I felt like her prayers would no longer be with me. I knew Oma was the only person who ever prayed for me every day! Through thick and thin I'd been able to count on those prayers for myself, my kids, step-kids, and grandkids, along with all our circumstances and concerns. Having to perform and minister at a Ladies Day, just days after my Oma's funeral, I apologized to my audience saying I couldn't possibly sing Grant's song, but as a tribute, I asked the ladies to listen to its powerful lyrics while it was played over the sound system from my laptop. The pastor's wife, approaching me after the event, said she too had struggled with such a loss. She then showed me that the Bible says, **The prayers of the saints are before the Lord forever. (Rev 8:4).** She assured me, on that special day that every prayer my Oma had ever prayed was still before the Lord! Wow, what a gift that simple word of encouragement was to me! This simple truth can empower us in our prayer life and demolish the nasty condemnation we might feel when we think we don't pray often enough! Thank you, Lord! Hallelujah! Eh?

Talking about the power of prayer, Bob has a remarkable story to tell of God's healing power in the lives of his son and his wife. Of all our children, Reagan and Alyssa were always the kid magnets! They were devastated when told they would not be able to have children of their own because Alyssa had cysts on her ovaries and endometriosis so bad. She had been a national level volleyball player and had not had regular menstrual cycles. They asked family and their church to pray for them, but those prayers had been to no avail. Awaking in the middle of the night months later, Reagan felt the Lord telling him to put his hand on his wife's belly and pray. Reagan did so and said he heard an audible snap as he prayed for healing.

Months later they moved and Alyssa found herself feeling out of sorts, sluggish and couldn't explain gaining about 5 pounds. The first round of numerous tests at the doctor showed nothing out of order. Days later, Alyssa returned to the doctor with grave concerns knowing something was happening and they continued the tests. The doctor entered the room to say the only thing they had discovered was that she was six months pregnant! LOL! They sent her for an ultrasound and the technician asked her why she hadn't realized she was pregnant sooner. Alyssa explained that she had been told she'd never have children due to her extreme case of endometriosis. The ultrasound tech said she knew exactly what that should look like having been diagnosed with the same condition herself! She showed Alyssa the screen and said, "There is absolutely no sign of endometriosis at all, nothing, but a healthy baby girl!"

Bob and I often speak about the authority we have in the realms of influence we've been given. The power of prayer is real in each of our lives. Reagan's great story is of a man taking leadership in his home as husband and father. Oma's prayers live on as the matriarch of our family. Consider that the Word of God says Jesus is interceding with us from Heaven, too and *there* is the hope we have!

One of my young grandsons was having terrible nightmares and was telling me he was afraid to go to sleep one night when I was babysitting. I told him how every scary thing has to flee in the name of Jesus. I said, "If you wake up having a bad dream you just say, "in Jesus' name, stop!" He practised diligently as I tucked him in. "Grandma!" he said the next morning. "You were right!! It worked!" Not too long afterward I overheard him telling his cousins the secret to getting rid of bad dreams! Now *that* is awesome!!

WHENEVER WE TURN TO THE RIGHT OR LEFT, WE WILL HEAR A VOICE BEHIND US SAYING, "THIS IS THE WAY. WALK IN IT." (ISAIAH 30:21) J<><

Anticipating a second winter visit to Arizona, I began wondering what our next year of southern living would look like. Through Arizona I knew God had extended our boundaries, enlarged our territories and grown wonderful, life-long friendships among the people we'd already met. Now Bob wanted to stretch things out a bit more, by being there for longer periods of time. I didn't know how I would honor God's call on my life to share my story and my music through ministry.

One night I lay in bed thinking about how the future would evolve. My parents had been facing some difficult issues and I wondered if I needed to stay 'home' to help them out. My dad had experienced a bout with colorectal cancer and was undergoing treatments and my mom had broken her foot and damaged the tendons. The foot had been basically severed from the ankle, leaving the foot dangling and requiring major surgery. Bob and I had tried to be with them as much as possible to alleviate some of the stress of care-giving from my sister and my family.

I was pondering and seeking God about what I was going to do that winter in Canada or Arizona as we were planning to go to AZ for February and March. I fell asleep asking God for absolute guidance. Suddenly, I woke up with two words before me: prophetic teaching. I had no idea what that was supposed to mean, but sensed God was showing me what I would be doing in Arizona. I got up and Googled "prophetic teaching in Arizona". What popped up on the screen turned out to be the name of a woman who had been a tremendous inspiration to me in previous years through her television ministry, Patricia King. Reading on her website, I discovered her Extreme Prophetic teaching ministry, had moved out of Canada and her office was now only forty minutes from where Bob and I lived in Mesa. It turned out that Ms King and her ministry, now called XP Media, were offering all sorts of conferences and classes within only ten minutes from our house. I got on the phone in the middle of the night and asked to register. I registered Bob and myself for every single one of them! LOL!!

Bob and I spent all of February and March attending these conferences and workshops. Each one proved to be a timely event where God confirmed to us what we needed to learn and impart in our own ministry. The special guests at these conferences spoke on the same things that Bob and I had sensed God leading us to do. We were being trained up during this period. For example, God had shown us one of the keys of our ministry was to teach on the virtues of positive living. Attending the LaRed & Global Priority sessions one day, exactly the same things were reiterated and a strategy for sharing them revealed!

Our ministry focus was strengthened as one of the leaders, Lance Wallnau, shared the philosophy of seven mountains of influence in society and our responsibility to take godly values into these 'kingdoms'! These mind molders are: Family, Education, Business, Government, Religion, Arts and Entertainment and Media. Bob and I realized that together, we had authority in all seven of those areas!

At these conference events, XP Media would often show little advertisements. The first one brought up singer songwriter, Julie Meyers, who had received a prophetic song about Media. As we watched on the big screen, she broke into song, "There's a new rose bloomin' in the desert..." about a new media army being raised up in the desert! I was excited and said, "Yeah! Cool! Go, God!"

We attended the next conference a few weeks later and all of a sudden, there was that same advertisement! At the end of the commercial, I felt the passion grow in me as my heart was touched. "Yes, God, please. We want to take back the kingdom of Media – in Hollywood and the Internet and local theatre!" I just knew that I knew I needed to be part of this in some way. I agreed but asked for more wisdom, clarity and direction. I sowed into this as I gave an offering that night! No clue what it might mean, I declared, "We are going to take back the kingdom of Media, this mountain molder of society! Yay, God! Go, God! Go, God!" I believed with the crowd gathered that together we'd see the end of what I considered to be Satan's control over media.

When Bob and I went to our final conference of the season, once again the same advertisement was played! Was God truly revealing that this was referring to me? I was being called into this media army! By the end of the commercial, I was weeping because I knew this was a call upon my life. My immediate reaction was that I felt I was too old for this type of thing! LOL! I decided not to panic and knew that God was in control. If He had a plan for me to be in media He would bring it to pass. Over the next weeks and months there was a constant prayer in my spirit, "Lord, please show me how this is going to evolve. Show me the truth of this calling on my life."

Bob and I were again participating in a Full Gospel Couples Advance in Camrose, Alberta. The possibility of 'changing the media world' was heavy on my heart one night as we visited over dinner with the couples gathered. I shared with everyone the vision of rising up in media, excitedly sharing the inspiration I had received! The next day, one of the couples approached us. They said the Lord had confirmed in their spirits the vision I had shared; that they felt called to sow into the 'media ministry' I was called to. As Bob opened the envelope extended, they said the $1000 they were giving should allow us to purchase a broadcast quality HD video camera! Bob was amazed and we felt so blessed. I wept. Bob began 'researching' the best camera to buy while the confirmation of God's plan grew in his heart, too.

Pondering the whole media thing including acting and film, I continued to pray. I realized perhaps there had been signs of this calling in my past! I had been the lead in **Anne of Green Gables** while in the eighth grade. Back in 1994, when my first marriage ended, I had been working at a television station and was inspired by ideas for shows. In fact, I had been on camera conducting interviews. Even back then, although I realized there was something being birthed in me I didn't know if I was qualified. I also wasn't sure I wanted to! Before I had a chance to work it all out, Satan blew it up big time when everything fell apart in 1994. Then I couldn't help but remember how when I was rebuilding my life, my mom and dad, brother and brother-in-law gave me a job in marketing and advertising. I was acting in the television commercials I wrote, as this little Dolores Detective character walking around, highlighting automotive parts and services.

Very gently the Lord was reminding me that just maybe this was who I was created to be. Had this been part of my destiny purposes all along?? A destiny that He had planned from before time began, but a destiny that had been stripped away from me? Was God now giving these things back to me? Hmmm...

IT'S ALWAYS EXCITING TO PONDER THE POSSIBILITY OF THINGS, NEVER DREAMED OF OR IMAGINED!! J<><

In the middle of summer we were again preparing to return to Arizona for the third winter. I decided to check XP Media online because I believed the Holy Spirit was showing me there was supposed to be some connection or involvement for me with XP Media again, possibly classes or conferences, etc. Bob had said he wasn't inclined to attend with me that year at all, so I should plan for myself alone. I discovered, that of all things, they were offering acting classes! Of course, I couldn't forget the "rose blooming in the desert" song Julie Meyers had sung and the way the Holy Spirit had moved in my spirit the year before!

At www.xpmedia.com, I discovered they had put together the most fantastic and comprehensive acting courses ever! Weekly classes, weekend intensive seminars, amazing coaches from the film and acting world, oh my! However, I was going to be on tour when the courses began and wondered if that would disqualify me. Or, maybe God was closing the door? I actually felt a wee bit of relief at that thought! Maybe He was just testing to see if I were willing? I made the necessary inquiries and asked whether missing the first two sessions would exclude me. Not a chance, I learned! We'd love to have you, they said. In fact, the two classes I'd be missing were all about "knowing you're called to the stage!!" "Missy", one of the acting coaches said, "Obviously, you have that figured out already as a performing artist! No problem!!" Now I was really nervous!

I arrived in Maricopa and kicked things off with a three-day intensive media boot camp. I met wonderful friends from all over the world who were all on the same page! It was remarkable! Really! It was amazing and awesome! A young guy sitting next to me informed me that he had been involved in a secular acting school for two years and had not learned as much as he did in the three days of XP Media boot camp. It was accelerated and powered by the Holy Spirit. Eyes are opened and ears in tune to hear the teaching. It is so clear and somehow as the Lord is given authority, it actually makes more sense to the student.

Even after a couple weeks in acting school, I still wasn't sure of how this was going to make a difference for me. I'd never seen myself as an actress! One evening in November we were doing cold reads. A cold read is an unpracticed audition where you are given a script and you just jump in and read it. The teacher had been a casting director for the old show **NYPD Blues**. Therefore, we were reading actual scripts from the old shows! Realizing I remembered some of the old episodes, I was astounded. It was almost a hoot! If only I could figure out why God wanted me there! As the reads went on, there was a lady in the room. At the end of the evening she was finally introduced as the Director of Vision Heaven Television in Glendale, Arizona. Linda Cross offered 'on-air' experience to the students! If any of us wanted or needed this experience, she had numerous projects on the go. Everyone was welcome to take part. There would be no pay, but we would get real on-air experience.

The thought of on-camera experience was awesome to me as one of my issues during acting class was that my coaches were often asking me to "bring it down just a little." I had always been taught as a stage performer, that everything had to be bigger than real, bigger than life. Those big smiles I smiled like crazy with the Continentals were WAY too much on the TV screen! After leaving class that evening, Linda and I had coffee together and I discovered that I was going to be able to get involved and work with Vision Heaven Television. I got to work on commercials and promos and felt it was really neat how it all came together.

The next spring, at the Women on the Frontlines conference held by XP Media, I was in the registration line-up for pastors and leaders when I met three women from England. Offering my services as a taxi driver, I felt so honored as friendships grew among my new friends and me. I also met folks from Africa, Australia and a beautiful couple who had immigrated to England from South Africa. God had definitely grown our ministry to the nations in ways I'd never imagined!!

Linda called and told me Visjon Norge in Norway had called and said they liked what I was doing for Vision Heaven in Arizona. The invitation was extended and all expenses would be paid if I would travel to minister with them. I would be interviewed, do interviews, perform live and have five music videos created while celebrating seven years of Christian television in Norway. This is where our story began on page 8 of this book. I am backstage and so humbled I'd been moved to tears and now before the camera. The applause was genuine! But you could suddenly hear a pin drop as the powerful lyrics filled the airwaves. The production staff was moved deeply as I sang the song I had written, *I Am There,* to as many as a million viewers that night in Scandinavia! Crazy, but true! Wonderful, and so profound!

When your heart is hurting for a love that's lost
Or rejection's reeling from a hardened heart
And the quiet tears don't seem to want to stop
I AM THERE.

When you're grieving deeply yet no one cares
Or you're baffled by the depth of love not shared
And the pain of loss tries to overwhelm
I AM THERE. I AM THERE.

And the love I have for you will never end
And the hope I offer you once more extends
To the deepest, darkest place within your soul.
I AM THERE. I AM THERE.

The sun will shine if you will lift your head
Rebuke the fear and pain in Jesus' name.
Strength and peace will fill that void within
And together we'll start to live in joy again.

You're not alone... No, I AM THERE.
Every moment of every day please know I care

Lives were being changed. As I shared my testimony, the call centre received numerous phone calls and people were led to the Lord. I was so humbled to see the ways God had accelerated a media career for me so quickly! He was using me and my gifts to bring people to the saving knowledge of His love and mercy. I was so honored and empowered to help change the media world for God's glory.

While I was in Norway, the invitation came to join Visjon Norge in Israel as the English commentator for the Feast of Tabernacles the following October. I began to pray again about this second opportunity to travel to Israel! Visjon Norge would *not* be able to pay for flights this time. As I gave the trip over to the Lord, I had a powerful sense that I was supposed to be going, but I said again, I needed a sign! Suddenly, I had a Skype call from England! The Princess Ministries would like me to come and minister with them in the UK. In fact, a Women's Conference was to be held, and they wanted me to be the keynote speaker! The weekend of the event was exactly the week before I would be in Israel! I took the invitation as confirmation that I'd be going overseas... first to England, then to Israel! LOL!

That spring, as we headed back to Canada, I felt I needed to take the new camera we had purchased and interview people on the streets. I knew I was called to build and grow my skills on camera and share the testimonies of people I would meet! I began to pray as to what I should do!

Jeanette Heshka suddenly came to mind. We'd met our friend at the first CGMA convention we'd attended in Yorkton. In fact, I remembered being so cold while I was there. The weather had turned chilly and I had not packed warm enough clothes so had been praying. I'd promised Bob and God that I was not going to spend money, BUT I needed a sweater, dear Lord! The next morning, Jeanette showed up at worship time with a green garbage bag in tow. "I hope you don't mind," she said. "I felt the Lord telling me to bring you something!" My eyes almost 'bugged out of my head' as Jeanette began unpacking sweaters and light jackets that I could borrow to match all my outfits that week! Jeanette became a beautiful friend to Bob and me and we stayed with her whenever we traveled through Yorkton. Bob often found little chores to do for her around the house, as she was on her own with her sight failing due to diabetes.

As I was pondering media and cameras and filming that upcoming summer, Jeanette's daughter suddenly came to mind! Immediate excitement and understanding grew as I remembered Michelle was just finishing a degree in film from the University of Regina. I connected with her and asked if she'd be interested in a short-term mission trip. The My Destiny Tour was born as the three of us travelled together! Bob and I came to love this amazing young woman and her remarkable gifts! Since then Bob and I launched our own channel on the XP Media Internet network believing God's media call on our lives was to expand. At www. xpmedia.com/channel/bobandjodifaith much of Michelle's work from that earlier tour can be viewed as we've begun revisiting the archived footage we gathered during that blessed trip! Although the video from Norway and Israel has been seen on Visjon Norge and Vision Heaven, it is now also highlighted on our new channel. They were extraordinary trips and I am so blessed to now share my work there with a greater international audience. The prayers of the people gathered from the many nations of the world to bless Israel are especially profound. I've been moved to tears knowing God has called me to bless His people. We believe these videos will bless you also!

One day as Charlotte and I were visiting at her place, working on this book, I received a phone call from a lay pastor living at Hecla Island, MB. It reminded me of how God connects people in such marvelous ways. It had been a number of years since we'd begun living in AZ during the winters. Following God's plans meant leaving hearth and home in Canada! Arizona had introduced us to ministry in Norway, England and Israel as well as Hecla Island! A neighbour at Venture Out told us we really should visit Hecla Island, north of the Gimli and Riverton area of Manitoba. She said, "I just know they'll love you guys there!" They were part of a historical community where people from Iceland had immigrated to this island on Canada's northern lakes. "In fact," she said, "we have this little church and it's a historical site. We have a wonderful pastor couple who take care of services there. Please contact them!"

I really wanted to honor my friend and take her up on this invitation. It took work to find the right contact info! It meant 'going where we'd never gone before!' But, today the pastors of that tiny little historic church have become wonderful friends to Bob and me. This terrific couple, who are called to do 'summer ministry' in the church there, arranged a ten-day tour for us from Riverton to Gimli, and all the way to Fisher Branch. We have become totally fantastic friends in the Lord. It is so special when we connect with others on a real heart level and we agree life is all about sharing God's love in a hurting world.

After Bob and I visited Hecla, John and Maxine became our first official retreat guests in our Holy Spirit-inspired 'cobalt blue cottage' in Arizona. The whole 'cobalt blue cottage' story is another one of the ordained-by-God blessings in our lives! I had my first vision of this home when I was in England for my first ministry tour! Celebrating the beauty of the English countryside, God laid a vision of a retreat house on my heart as I took photos of Elaine's potted red geraniums in her huge cobalt blue pottery planters. As I took the last photo, I saw this set of pictures in a home I didn't recognize. I claimed the promise and began to collect blue souvenirs while I traveled for the home I knew I was going to have one day!

Bob's biological father, Percy, passed away and left a small legacy for him. Very unexpectedly, we received a call from neighbors in AZ asking whether we'd like to purchase their home right next door to ours in Venture Out. Bob took the money received from his father's estate and invested it in the property. I painted and redecorated and the home was transformed into the beautiful 'cobalt blue cottage' I had dreamed of. Hosting guests in AZ, especially those who have hosted us throughout our years on the road, has been a lovely blessing! We love being able to share our hospitality with those who visit us there.

God wants to give us the desires of our heart! J<><

I firmly believe that God cares about every detail of our lives not just the major and difficult circumstances we experience. Although unconscious or unmentioned, I believe these things are the 'desires of our heart.'

Ironically, Bob shares a testimony about me and my shoes. Every time he turns around, he thinks I'm wearing a new pair. Whether they are new or used doesn't matter. Even though I buy him $150 walking shoes and buy myself $3 flip-flops, they are equal in Bob's view. Eventually, in order to keep the peace, I decided to honor my husband and not buy another pair of shoes, period!

When we arrived at the CGMA convention a few weeks later, our lovely friend, Louise Klein, approached me. She said, "I think I have something for you. What size shoes do you wear?" She went to her car and returned with the most beautiful pair of sandals. She'd found them at a garage sale and believed they'd fit someone perfectly! They did! On stage that night I told everybody the entire story, concluding with my opinion of how much God loves me. He got me a new pair of shoes in spite of me or Bob! Even though I didn't pay one cent for them, Bob was still exasperated. BUT all that turned around later in the week when he got up to share what life was like as my manager! He smiled and simply said, "I manage Jodi and her SHOES!" Everyone laughed including Bob as he later received the Manager of the Year Silver Heart Award.

God has shown me that we need to share these little stories from our lives, those times when we know God showed up!! So few people know this living, caring, genuinely interested and engaged God we serve!

Bob and I were visiting a hospitable couple in the Manitou Beach, SK area. Our hostess served us with their beautiful wedding china and we told her about ours. As we planned to be married, we had decided we didn't want any gifts. Other couples that had married for a second time or later in life advised us, however, to pick something or end up with tons of stuff we really didn't need. After much consideration, Bob and I decided to register at Stokes. Neither of us had owned nice china, wine glasses or crystal. We were so blessed to receive exactly what we'd chose!

Three years later as we packed for the move to Lafleche we sold the large, beautiful dining room table that seated twenty people and the matching china cabinet that held our wedding china. As I was packing I really felt that it just wasn't fair. I loved to entertain and be hospitable and now it was all being taken away.

Bob said, "Don't worry about it. God will give you another china cabinet someday."

"Oh, whatever! You better promise me that you will get me a new china cabinet," I mumbled through my tears.

We moved from that 2000+ sq. ft. 5-bedroom home into the 1000 sq. ft. teacherage and then downsized again to our present, tiny 825 sq. ft. cottage. Contemplating the move here, I looked at the unopened bins full of china and crystal and decided to put them into our garage sale. After all we knew were going to remain missionaries and have no use for china. Bob was mortified and asked what I thought I was doing. I replied, "Well, we'll never have a china cabinet again and there's no place to put all of this stuff. Besides, we won't need it anyways."

"You don't know that for sure. We aren't sure what God has in mind," Bob told me.

Relating the story, we told our hostess how just a few years later the search began to find a home in AZ. We walked into a home and the first thing I saw was this wall-to-wall china cabinet. I felt like crying. After all, by this time I had totally forgotten about the china cabinet I had wanted. God knew this desire of my heart, not only to have my china and crystal, but also to use them and my gifts of hospitality). To this day, anybody that visits our home in Venture Out is served on our wedding china.

After sharing my story about how God cares about all the little things in our lives, our hostess did not agree. In fact, she suggested the telling of the story was my way of manipulating the truth to make it seem that God cares about such things! I remember being astonished by her dismissive reaction. It is sad to us, that there are so many people in the world who don't know God in this intimate way. A desire of Bob's heart and mine is that we can reach people and help them understand this personal relationship.

Immersed in a life of singing and sharing, I have realized I was created for this, for such a time as this! The lack of fulfillment is gone and the purpose I had been searching for now found. My hearts desires fulfilled, I trust God is speaking through me. I see Bob as a spiritual barometer indicating whether the Holy Spirit is getting through and using what I am saying for His purposes. Right from the beginning of our ministry his discernment and deep sensitivity to God would move him to tears. At times, as I see him at the back of the room, he is literally sobbing. He knows me best and is always in awe of how God uses my gifts and abilities.

Destiny and Her Happy Sword! J<><

Another example of prophetic promises over my life continues to intrigue me. As I mentioned, Patricia King is one of my spiritual mentors and an example of a frontline 'warrior'. She is also a woman who has been used by God to minister to me when I've been in the midst of something major happening in my life. Watching her show on TV years ago, or seeing her in person today, I would hear the exact words that I needed at that particular time. God has worked through her in amazing ways.

When I was in the audience at one of her events, Patricia came off the stage, down the aisle and spoke a message directly to me. She cut-off word curses that had been spoken over me. It brought me to tears and gave me confirmation and strength not to give up. While editing this book, I found our ministry newsletter dated March 2010. This excerpt from that newsletter including the transcript of Patricia's words is still relevant for today:

"I learned recently there is no word for coincidence in the Hebrew language. Coincidences are NOT from the Lord!! Understanding that has been pretty cool for me as I've learned to embrace every moment as a destiny moment! Today!! When I think of our supporters and ministry friends – each and everyone was a divine appointment...a God orchestrated encounter – again no coincidences there!

My advice to each of you is to get excited about who God may put in your path today! Talk to people! Engage and reach out!! Be sure you don't overlook the destiny purpose attached to these moments or the ways chance encounters may lead to amazing opportunities, never dreamed of or imagined!

We are also being reminded that there may be some folks in our circle who don't understand the call on our lives. As we move forward, we ask you to please agree with us that, "His Will Be Done". These are the words God spoke over me through Patricia King:

"The Lord says that there's been a stirring on the inside of your heart in these days and I see intercession, intercession and warfare… intercession and warfare and the Lord says that out of your belly shall flow rivers of living water, but He says that there's been some turmoil within over some things and there are some situations and even some words that have even acted like curses against you that have come and pierced you in the spirit and you've been wondering why can't I break through, and why can't I run, and why can't I rise up in stronger ways, why can't I soar like how I see in my spirit? And the Lord says that this night, this night that there's a release over you and the Lord declares over you that no weapon formed against you prospers and every tongue that has risen up against you in judgment and every word is condemned tonight in the name of Jesus and the Lord says, You are blessed, you are blessed, you are blessed, you are blessed, and who God has blessed no words can curse. And in the name of Jesus I say, open up ye gates, open up ye gates and let the King of Glory… let the King of Glory come in… (Quiet, rest…)

Whoooo… (Laughter!!) I see a happy sword in your hand… It's a sword of war, but it's a happy sword! It's not the kind of warfare that's a grueling warfare… it's like the kind of warfare that says, Yippee!! Let's go get a giant's head! It's a happy sword! And the Lord says, It's a happy sword!! Heehee!!"

As I drove down the road later that evening, I got a vision of a little girl with a huge sword. As the sweet characters appeared, I named them "Destiny and Her Happy Sword". Over the days that followed, every time I turned around more visions of characters appeared as though from an animated series that I might work on creating. Destiny had these big boots. She was stomping across the tops of mountains! She and the Happy Sword appeared to be larger than life!

This download happened at the time I was in film and acting school. It seemed that it was a time of creativity and writing being birthed. In my brain I could see four or five possible movies to be done. All the concepts were very vivid in my mind and I can easily retell the stories.

Not very long afterward, I was sitting in the hot tub with my friend from Manitoba as she and her husband had come to visit us in Arizona.

As we visited, I began telling her the story of **Destiny and Her Happy Sword**; the happy sword being the Word of God. I told her of the great vision of these programs being created and that all I was missing was an animator. Pamela Funk told me that her son, Gideon, was an animator! Totally cool! He was barely out of high school, but his great dream was to be an animator. Through Facebook, I hooked up with Gideon and almost immediately the little characters I'd envisioned began to come to life through his pencil!

AND DARLIN' LONG AS YOU HAVE BREATH,
YOU'RE NOT FINISHED YET! J<><

The Lord has often got me singing my old jingle... singing it to myself,
prophetically decreeing and declaring His plans and purposes for my life
are not done yet! Often I feel the power of the Holy Spirit lift me right
out of discouragement and anxiety as I sing it! I'm moved to tears as I
think about how much impact the song has had in ministry.

Bob and I had performed at the Moosehorn Gospel Jamboree. In
addition to finding our hearts blessed with wonderful new friendships,
we celebrated great CD sales, too! Months later, I received a letter from a
young student in the Interlake area of Manitoba. In a school assignment,
they'd been asked to recall a song that they liked and answer two questions! "What did the lyrics say?" and "What did the words mean to them?"
I was blown away as I read how this little foster child had felt such huge
encouragement and hope for her future because of the words God had
given me for my little jingle!"

Years later, Bob and I performed at a concert in Choiceland, SK for
about twenty ladies who were up in years. They were mostly the mothers
of the kids that Bob had taught in the area in the 1970's. In this gathering,
there was also a younger lady present. She was a single mom and had been
wondering what life really had to offer someone like her. Unbeknownst
to me, discouragement had been heavy on her heart. I knew, beyond a
shadow of a doubt, that she needed to hear the lyrics of **Lady of Destiny**.
As I gave her the Now Is The Time album, I said, "There is so much powerful truth in this album and it is all for you. I just know God is going to
bless you." Bob and I chatted with her and prayed together with her. We
hadn't sung many of the songs from that album that night because we'd

been invited to entertain rather than minister. It was worth the entire trip to be able to give it to her and to tell her she was a 'lady of destiny' and, that as long she had breath, God was not finished with her yet.

The Bible says, "We overcome by the blood of the Lamb and the word of our testimony." (Revelations 12:11) J<><

The story of the **Now Is The Time** album and how it came to be is a great testimony of God's faithfulness I have had to remind myself of often. These stories of God showing up are so important when we're going through tough times! God provided! Exactly when needed, the cheque for $5,000 was there! Then when the amount of $15,000 was needed, it was there! In the Bible it says that the enemy comes to "steal, kill and destroy!" Unfortunately, the next chapter in the **Now Is The Time** story is pretty brutal in many ways.

The company I signed the deal with was not Universal Music at all. In reality, it was a distributor for Universal Music. D2 Records/IKON Records, working on behalf of Universal, had taken all of my money but had manufactured only the first five hundred of the five thousand CDs we'd paid for. They assured me they would make more as needed. According to the contract I signed, it was essential for me to set up my calendar for the next year including a promotional plan. In years gone by, the manager of upcoming stars like Elvis Presley walked into a radio station and gave them $5 to play his tunes. That's still pretty much how it works today. It's very difficult to get radio airplay time, particularly in the country gospel genre and especially in Canada. I asked the record company if they could give me the promised list of their radio stations. They were to supply some radio spots where the jingle I had written and recorded would be used! Since that was the main inspiration and purpose for *Lady of Destiny* I was excited about that! I would then create a tour in the communities where those stations were located. I discovered to my horror that there was no list! There was absolutely nothing! We sold out of the first five hundred CDs without D2 honoring any of their commitments. We insisted that they send us another thousand, which they did.

The whole deal fell apart over the years that followed. I left message after message on a voicemail system with never a call returned! I began to receive phone calls from other artists asking about my deal with D2 Records. Everyone's stories were the same. These other artists wondered what D2 was doing for me and whether I'd be willing to join a lawsuit. I tried to get in touch with my A & R guy, but he was no longer available because he was on the road with an up-and-coming artist. It was as though, these people just took my money and ran. Although my inventory of the album was running out again and I desperately needed more, it was hard to imagine how that was going to happen. Even though both parties involved had signed a legal agreement, it wasn't being upheld. Finally, I talked to the actual owner of D2 and he said, "Uh yeah, I'm kinda broke." He had gone to the States with a movie distribution deal. While there he encountered health issues that landed him in the hospital with no health insurance. Trying my hardest to believe his story and his promise that he would be good for the agreement, I waited, but nothing happened!

The dishonored deal affected our marriage as Bob was very angry and rightfully so. He felt I had been taken. I still believe that God had given me signs and the deal was supposed to be a God story! Nowhere in the Bible does it say the world is going to treat us right, though. It says pretty much the opposite, but it also says that God will be there to sustain us through the trials.

The $15,000 was gone and so we started praying about the situation and what we were supposed to do. Bob is as tenacious as a bulldog and every few months would tell me to email or call that guy to find out when he was going to send the CDs. I would begrudgingly do so. Hearing no answer, I must admit I had pretty much given up on it. With the five-year contract about to expire Bob and I were distressed! The whole situation was pretty pathetic in reality!

As Charlotte and I worked on the book in July of 2012 I felt desperately depressed over our finances. It was just brutal! I shared the story of the broken deal and how our ministry life hadn't been financially rewarding. We had been able to cover our expenses, but even that had begun to shift in the past years of economic decline. The doomsday reports on the news said we were all going broke! With fear running rampant, the 'with-holding spirit' was attacking people. I felt as though we'd sold out for Jesus and done all we could to serve Him. I felt like we'd given up everything but it was getting more and more difficult financially! There was almost no money coming into our ministry and the cost of fuel was increasing, etc. Where would the money come from to publish this book? A new song list was growing but there was no money to finish another album. Bob and I were both discouraged. Being on the road for eight years had been exhausting for him. He would often remind me that he is ten years older than I am. It had indeed been hard for both of us!

I was at a place where I was telling God that I needed a sign if we were supposed to be done with ministry. Most of my CDs were gone. I would be happy to hang up our traveling shoes and spend time with our seven children and the seventeen grandchildren we had at the time. Being at home in our little town of Lafleche was also appealing because we didn't know half the people living there anymore. Maybe this would be our last year on the road!

On August 10, 2012, we were driving down the road in Nova Scotia. "Ding!" Out of the blue, there was a text message from Rui deSylva, the owner of D2 Records. "I want you to know that I just ordered 1,000 CDs and they will be delivered to you by next week." We were astounded. It was such a shock we almost had to pull over on the side of the road! I realized that deep down I had really been hoping we could retire but this was a major sign that God wasn't done with us yet. Now we were asking God to show us what He wanted us to do next. Out of Bob's mouth came these words, "Maybe we need to do that new album." I had started three songs at a studio in Calgary but they'd been on hold for a while.

Even though we had 3500 copies of the **Now Is The Time** album still coming to us, it was almost five years old. In the industry, that can be a bit of a problem. If we highlighted a new album in concert, the old one could become a secondary seller perhaps? We could sell the new one for $20 and offer the old one for an extra $5 or $10 and try to get our investment out of it! During the last few years, we'd started a list of new songs we'd been singing! If another album ever came to be we knew these songs would have to be included. Although deep down we'd wondered if that would ever happen, suddenly we were getting excited! Thank you, Lord! We remembered the verse, **God will restore the years the locust has eaten!** (Joel 2:25) We chose to claim this promise over this situation! The plan for a new album began to grow.

This tour included performing at the Hank Snow Country Music Festival in Bridgewater, Nova Scotia for the second time. I was required to have live music accompaniment. The guitar player I had contracted was Hank Middleton and he absolutely loved my story. While rehearsing I shared how I was forbidden to sing for over seventeen years and the whole thing about not wanting to sing country music. LOL! I shared how God had taken my songs to over fifty countries of the world. I told him it was awesome to be back in Bridgewater celebrating the fifth anniversary of working with the Work for Widows project. Upon hearing the story of the widows, Hank asked whether I'd consider singing a song he had written since it reminded him so much of my message! I listened to it and liked it. He gave me a copy of his powerful song and Bob thought it was great, too. Adding *Eagle's Wings* to my repertoire for the weekend, I asked whether we could try to get into the studio and record it together. He said he had a better idea.

I thought Hank Middleton was the best guitar player I had ever heard next to Eddy Rigetti, but he said he knew a guy who played even better. In fact, he said, a completed soundtrack for *Eagle's Wings* was sitting at his friend's studio and I was welcome to use it! Hank called his friend to see if he might be available. Miraculously, he was. Some people would say this is an amazing coincidence, but I know it was totally God! It had been difficult being in Nova Scotia for a six-week tour and having to cover expenses. Bookings were needed, but nothing had been arranged for the entire week of September 10th – 17th. It was weird. It was festival season and should have been simple to get bookings. In hindsight, I could see perfectly how God made sure that week was wide open. Jude Pelley, Hank's talented friend at Alone Stone Productions in West Dublin, NS was available *that* entire week as well. Exactly, one month after the call from D2 Records on August 10, we were in studio recording the new CD. The studio in Calgary sent the tracks for the tunes we'd started there and we were able to be in studio every single day! I had a line of credit I used but we believed the money would come in!

Saying farewell to Jude, Bob and I flew to England where I was booked to speak at a women's conference. There I reunited with my friends Elaine and Bernie Armstrong. Bernie had just composed a wonderful theme song for the conference, ***Abundant Love, Abundant Life!*** The Holy Spirit showed me that this song should be on the new album. I'd felt the same way about another of Bernie's songs, ***Arise, Shine,*** which I had heard the previous year. I was in the studio of John Perry in Hayworths Heath, West Sussex recording those two songs for the album a week later! LOL!

God put each one of us together in such an unbelievable way! The title track (which Jude helped me finish) and the entire album epitomize the power of encouraging and believing in one another... ***Hands United!***

You've come so very far, through sunshine and rain
Bruised and battle-scarred, stronger from so much pain...
Although you've lost it all, you've arrived standing tall...
Free to believe, hands united...

Step up to the wall, and lift up your hands
Believe in your dreams coming true as you stand...
Beside the open door, forgotten no more...
Free to believe, hands united

Hands united, hands united
Free to believe, hands united

Shake off your weary chains, give life to your dreams
Love is what remains, after all that you've seen
In spite of it all, you've arrived standing tall...
Free to believe, hands united

All of us worked together and my vision for ministry was restored and renewed! During the tough season we were in, I needed that! We selected twelve songs and **Hands United,** my fifth album, was mastered in British Columbia and released in January 2014. Talk about universal music! It was a global project, from Calgary to Nova Scotia to England to British Columbia. The album is dedicated to the Work For Widows project. It is also a tribute to those who are willing to share their stories of overcoming the schemes of an enemy who comes to "steal and kill and destroy" (Romans 10:10) A little late, but better than anything we could have hoped for, the new album will sell alongside the **Now Is The Time** and **Second Chance** albums! Surprisingly, **Hands United** was nominated as the 2014 Country Gospel Album of the Year by the Saskatchewan Country Music Association.

WE HAVE AN ENEMY WHO DESIRES TO STOP
US IN OUR TRACKS AND WILL 'STEAL, KILL
AND DESTROY' IN ORDER TO DO SO! J<><

Since receiving my first CGMA awards, Bob and I have put out a 'fleece' each year. We ask God if it is His will for us to go to Branson to represent Canada at the international convention. We want to be a part of the family of believers gathering there every year and know we would be uplifted and encouraged if we did attend. We have supported the CGMA in Canada and have watched our ministry grow with the credibility we've received from our national awards. Representing Canada, I would be eligible for international recognition but have waited on the Lord to show us whether it's His will to attend the Branson event. Many times the only booking we'd get, even a year in advance, was at the exact time of the convention in Branson so we'd know it wasn't His will for us to go. We prayed, "Father, if it is Your will for us to attend International, please allow us to receive a performance award and we'll go". If we didn't receive a performance award we chose to believe it simply wasn't His will. However, almost every year, after the voting was concluded, we'd have people say "I wanted to vote for you... I thought I should vote for you but didn't think that made sense... Obviously you don't need another award! You two are obviously well on your way with your ministry/career..." Was it possible God's will for our lives was sabotaged?

On another occasion, I was the keynote speaker at a women's conference. I interjected a few songs here and there and felt my presentation had gone well. Many women said they'd been very inspired and touched. Staying back until the very end, a lady asked to speak to me. As she thanked me, she said she had been so moved by all she had heard, but that it actually made her angry! As the woman shared her heart I learned she had wanted to invite me to be a speaker at their church's women's retreat years before! She'd heard about my budding ministry and felt God was showing her that I was His choice for speaker. She knew another woman, who had been the speaker at a retreat where I was singing. She'd called that lady to ask for my contact information. I felt sick to my stomach as I heard how this speaker said she could *not* recommend me at all because she didn't feel I was qualified! She said I was "too shallow, immature in ministry, etc. etc. etc." The woman in front of me felt God's plans for her group had been stolen. God's grace and mercy flowed that day as His love filled me. I had to apply and exemplify Christ's forgiveness. I was able to minister to the lady as we both asked for forgiveness and protection from the spirit of offense and hurt. I must admit that I have wondered since how many times *that* has happened!

Another beautiful friend said to me one day, "I love your newsletters and pray for you all the time but, Jodi, you need to know people are reading them and instead of praying for you, are belittling you, your reports, your hopes and your dreams! They are making fun of everything you are doing! It's horrible! You think they're your prayer partners but they are speaking word curses over you!" Talk about the enemy "killing, stealing and destroying!" I actually quit sending out prayer letters for a time after that!

Sometimes I have wondered why these stories have been revealed to us. There is no way to know whether the circumstances have changed and quite frankly, I might have preferred *not* to know what others have said or done. While ministering to others who have been hurt by people in the church, I've been reminded of how we have overcome some of these experiences. "Grace, grace, God's grace" has given me the ability to forgive the hurts and hardships. I choose to be obedient to continue to try to serve the Lord regardless. Unfortunately as Christians, we are known as the only army who shoot our own soldiers! I've learned to seek validation from God, not man. I remember those who have gone on before us! "Oh Lord, help me *not* to cry… Help me *not* to get angry or offended or worse to throw in the towel… Keep us strong, please!"

Not long ago, I was praying as to whether I should quit telling my story. Some people were suggesting I was being too transparent and enough had been said. In the midst of that, I shared the difficulties Bob and I were having on a personal level with my friend. Suddenly she said, "Thank you! I have been s-o-o encouraged! It's crazy! But the way you simply tell your story and share the struggles... like it's no big deal! Saying, you'll survive!" she said, "It's been just awesome! I feel so much more hope!" LOL! I recently read a commentary, which spoke to my heart! Here's what the Lord gave me: "*The storyline of your life is well established, yet not always well known. The struggles and challenges you've faced and overcome are worth celebrating and talking about. When you're transparent with others and tell your story you give them opportunity.*" Dr. Mark Chironna

We have personally been honored to be part of the global work of The Gideons International. So often the theme scripture verse chosen by their ministry has precisely "fit" our own ministry and vision! The "pressing toward the mark" mantra has been a constant whisper in our ears since it was their theme verse many years ago, when Bob's and my ministry was little more than a kindling flame. I love this verse, especially in the Message version! From Hebrews 12:1-3 it is titled, "Discipline in a Long-Distance Race"

Do you see what this means—all these pioneers who blazed the way, all these veterans cheering us on? It means we'd better get on with it. Strip down, start running—and never quit! No extra spiritual fat, no parasitic sins. Keep your eyes on *Jesus*, who both began and finished this race we're in. Study how he did it. Because he never lost sight of where he was headed—that exhilarating finish in and with God—he could put up with anything along the way: Cross, shame, whatever. And now he's *there*, in the place of honor, right alongside God. When you find yourselves flagging in your faith, go over that story again, item by item, that long litany of hostility he plowed through. *That* will shoot adrenaline into your souls!

YOU WANT ME TO SPEAK UP AND TAKE A STAND,
DEAR LORD?
HMMMM... I FEEL THE RIGHTEOUSNESS RISING! J<><

Without being conscious of it, God had placed a burden on me to advocate for the victims of the sex trade and create awareness about the human trafficking issue. The Work For Widows Project began as a way to offer hope to those without it! Their motto became, Help Us, Help Them, Help Themselves. In Sri Lanka, widows felt they had no choice but to sell themselves and their own children. The program stopped human trafficking as alternative income was generated through the sale of their beaded items. Because of my involvement, I discovered I have governmental authority in the realm of human trafficking because we're not just talking about it, but being actively engaged. When I'm standing out in the sweltering heat and high humidity for hours and sell only three or four pieces of jewelry, it is easy to wonder whether it's really worth it. I have to rebuke myself because it *is* worth it! The money and awareness is helping a widow and orphan, and that is exactly what Jesus told us to do.

As I drove down the road one day listening to an instrumental piece by Joshua Mills (an incredible pianist), I had another vision.. This time though it had a horrible storyline. Moved to tears, I found myself narrating this story aloud as he played: *A rebellious young woman is at the mall food court. Lured outside with sweet lies and promises she is abducted. Over the course of several days she is sexually abused by numerous men. A beautiful creative song begins rising up in me and flowing over Joshua's music as I hear myself prophesying healing over the woman in the video.*

Jesus Loves you, washes you clean,
Jesus loves you no matter where you've been.
Mercies new he'll wash you white as snow,
Step by step, wherever you go...

As I arrived at Vision Heaven Television in Glendale the day after receiving the vision, song and inspiration for this message, I found myself singing it and 'seeing' it over and over again. Linda received a phone call from Norway in the middle of our photo shoot. The story idea resonating in my head, I sat down to write it out. It would be called CLEAN. When Linda got off the phone, she read my narrative on the topic of human trafficking. The Holy Spirit was prompting me to film the project right then and there. I asked Linda if it was even possible. We turned the cameras on and I narrated the story to the song I'd heard. Within moments it was 'in the can'. Now what, Lord? Linda knew she would show it on Vision Heaven.

I was able to get in touch with Joshua Mills to ask his permission to use his song. He told me most definitely. After being at Vision Heaven all day, I had a planned conference call with my animator, Gideon Funk, who had been contracted to work on **Destiny and The Happy Sword**. I'd previously shared the concept and he and I planned to discuss the illustrations he had drawn and sent. Completely distracted, I shared with Gideon the incredible happenings of the previous twenty-four hours.

Gideon was astounded and said, "Are you kidding me? God just showed me on Sunday that I was supposed to do a project on human trafficking!" LOL! Through the awesome avenue of technology, Linda was able to upload a copy of the video we had created and send it to Gideon. He then produced an animated version of the story. By having it done in animated form, we knew the story was more palatable. The truth of human trafficking is ugly, something that the world has difficulty accepting! For example, in 2009 over 260,000 children were abducted in the United States alone. Parents often think their child has run away when in actuality he/she was kidnapped. During Super Bowl 2014, law enforcement busted a prostitution ring offering 13–17 year-old children for sale. Many of these were US citizens reported missing by family members.

Incidentally, Gideon submitted the video to the XP MEDIA Film Festival. I was stunned when we never heard anything back because it was such an amazing piece of work. We soon discovered that he had put the *wrong address* on the package and it was never received. I had to choose to believe that God still had a plan for the video and that His timing is always perfect. The Lord *will* restore what the locust has eaten. He is the Restorer! When Gideon felt God calling him to attend animation school, he emailed asking me to write him a reference letter because of the CLEAN project. Gideon was accepted into the Vancouver Animation School on the basis of the project which he'd done for us. He graduated in the spring of 2012.

What a legacy!
The power of a Grandmother's prayers! J<><

In her well-read and worn German Bible, my Oma had a bookmark. On the one side was the 'multiplication table' written in Oma's uniquely interesting Russian-Canadian penmanship. My nephew Spencer once asked her what it meant. Oma said, "If you don't use em, you lose 'em." She proceeded to tell Spencer how she would recite them daily. On the reverse side of that bookmark was a list of all her children, grandchildren, great-grandchildren, the significant others of each and even the step-children and step-grands who she prayed for daily 'by name'. As new ones were born there names got added to the bottom of that list.

I would often laugh out loud as I testified to the fact that I was celebrating a wonderful, amazing and exciting life today because God answered my Grandmother's prayers. It is because of this special lady that Bob and I like to sing the song *Bring Back The Days When Grandmas Would Pray,* written by Grant Farmer of Medicine Hat, AB. In my own experience and through the composer's words a wonderful truth is shared. Grandmas are often the ones who never give up on their loved ones even "when we err and go our own way". "Can you just imagine," I often ask my audience, "the prayer beads that have been held and the prayers that have gone up, the hearts cry from generations of grandmothers that have been heard by the Lord?" My third album was ready to go to press the day I heard that song for the very first time in 2006. The album called **Faith, Family and Friends** was to be a tribute to the kinds of things songs were written about... love and life... angels and heaven and... Grandmas!! A group opening for me sang that song and I whispered to Bob through my tears, "We have to add this song to the album!" Bob agreed, but wondered how to contact Grant. Swallowing my tears, I stepped onto the stage and asked for permission to pray. I told the audience how much the song had meant to me. Then I introduced them to my beloved Oma who sat in the crowd, while I dedicated the entire concert to her!

Bring back the days Lord when Grandmas would pray
Bring back the children who've erred and gone the wrong way
Let's tell the story that Jesus saves
Bring back the days Lord when Grandmas would pray

How well do I remember… How well do I recall
My grandma's faded bible and the verses on her wall…
Her hands tightly folded as to Jesus she did call
A heart that sounded broken as the tears began to fall

Bring back the days Lord when Grandmas would pray

In case you all still need proof that God cares about these kinds of things in our lives, the next day as Bob and I went to the bank before leaving town, who should happen to be in front of us at the ATM but none other than Grant Farmer – the composer! Not only did he give us absolute permission to sing the song, but also to include it on our upcoming album! You've gotta' love it, eh! LOL! It's just s-o-o cool. It's also supernatural proof that God was in charge of the outrageously exciting and humbling music career that seemed to unfold right before our eyes! The song has become a fan favorite! In jamborees and festivals we will often have to sing it every set because people love it and request it so often. It has been a powerful inspiration to me as I know the prayers my Oma prayed were answered.

But the song also speaks to being very intentional about being involved in the lives of those around us. One thing my Oma did was keep on serving and ministering right until her last breath. She read the bible everyday and spent her time engaged in the lives of those around her. My children and extended family were all impacted by her generosity and care.

In Canada today, I know we are called to see a generation of mentors rise up and be the catalyst for the change we *need* to see in the world!

Passion continues to grow for Bob and me as we pray for the church to 'get up and get doing', rather than being a people filled with apathy and mediocrity. This zeal leaves me in tears at times. Where's the abundant life? Where's the joy? I try to be so gentle and discreet in motivating others to get involved and do something. After all, God must be grieving greatly for a church that is just not doing enough. Pastors have been heard to say 10% of the people give 90% of the finances and 90% of the volunteer time. An old cliché has become, "If you want something done, ask someone who is already busy!" The problem is Bob and I are meeting more and more people who want to check out saying we're tired, too busy, or too frustrated. Too often we hear people say, "Our needs are not being met." Instead, we pray they will learn to ask, "How can I serve?"

Being 'grandparents' to the children we meet in the highways and byways is a huge part of the ministry Bob and I feel called to also. As recipients of the 2013 Canadian Children's Ministry of The Year from the CGMA, we know God is expecting us to mentor children! Animal balloons and music in the park go a long way toward helping with that call! Every time we sing at a festival, do face-painting, prophetic art or make an animal balloon, we know God is opening a door. We take these opportunities to speak life and purpose into the hearts and minds of the children we meet *and* their family members. For example, Bob's 'Jonah inside the whale' balloon art is a great reminder that God doesn't want us to say no to going where He wants us to go! He wants us to say, "Yes, I want to change the world!"

We cry out every time we hear of another death by suicide or violence among our young people today! The Bible warns us that the condition of the human heart will lead us to hopelessness and desperation. Fear and loneliness also permeate our society today. It is essential that each one of us become a mentor, engaged in the discipleship of others! No one gets to check out. Our forty-plus generation *will* be held accountable by God for the ways we have abandoned the younger generations. Bob and I feel called to see our generation rise up to believe "it takes a village to raise a child!" We are so convinced of this obligation I auditioned on **Dragon's Den**, to beg for finances to accomplish this mandate!

Being His love and light in the world around us remains a huge part of the message Bob and I have been given to share! *How* to share the message is challenging and constantly changing! We received the Canadian CGMA Media Personality Of The Year award in 2013 for our work in television and media. The Jodi Faith Show was just renewed for a third season on Shaw Cable in Saskatchewan, while it was renewed for a second season on Access Television also. We are sharing the stories of those we meet, ordinary people with stories to tell! You can see some of our ministry on YouTube and our website, but sincerely, I am most excited about the potential of the XPMedia channel. Bob is most excited about traveling the Internet highway more and *not* having to pay over $5.00 for a gallon for diesel anymore! LOL! Sharing testimony and song so *you* can share it with others, XPMedia offers a potential viewership of thirty million a month!! Please see the channel at www.xpmedia.com/channel/bobandjodifaith. Hallelujah!

Bob and I heartily invite *you* to join us in sharing God's love in the hurting world! God has placed you exactly where He needs you to be 'for such a time as this'! Step up and become a mentor to someone. Share *your* experiences. Testify to the truth of the God who has shown up faithful in your life, especially in the small, everyday sorts of ways! The world needs to know God is real to you! The world around you may be desperately searching for hope, purpose, spiritual truth, peace and tranquility and *you* are right there, a living example of the truth that can set us free!

I have so much for you to do but you
must "Ask, Seek and Knock!" J<><

For a long time I've known something startling which is that mortal man cannot read my mind! LOL! Years ago I honestly thought if it's God's will for me 'to sing, or speak, or pray, serve, help or organize, someone would ask me!' Sheepishly, I now admit, I actually can't find that in the Bible! LOL! In the American Standard Version of the Word of God it says **"Ask, and it will be given to you; seek, and you will find; knock, and it will be opened to you."** (Matthew 7:7) The Message version says it all the more clearly: **7-11"Don't bargain with God. Be direct. Ask for what you need. This isn't a cat-and-mouse, hide-and-seek game we're in. If your child asks for bread, do you trick him with sawdust? If he asks for fish, do you scare him with a live snake on his plate? As bad as you are, you wouldn't think of such a thing. You're at least decent to your own children. So don't you think the God who conceived you in love will be even better?"**

This concept was revealed in a pivotal moment a year or so after Bob and I were married. As you know, he was always encouraging me to sing and wanted to hear me sing solos! I had just discovered a moving new song called **How Beautiful.** It was a tribute to the actual love of Jesus in our world and a song of honor for the body of Christ operating in the world today. Practicing with the worship team one evening, I sensed I was supposed to sing it as a solo. When I discovered communion was to be served that Sunday during both services, I was sure! I just loved my worship pastor, Randy Feere, and was sure he would ask me to sing that Sunday! I was so disappointed when not only did he not invite me to sing, but worse yet, the pastor used the exact words repeated in my lyrics as his segue into the communion service! I was almost sick to my stomach as I realized I *should* have been singing! My song choice would have been right on point, a perfect complement to a perfect service, if only he had asked me! Quite frankly, indignation began to rise up in me!

The Holy Spirit stepped in quickly and quietly, like a two-edged sword perhaps? I began to repent for the judgment that had so quickly tried to rear its ugly head! It wasn't Pastor Randy's fault! He couldn't read my mind. The Holy Spirit spoke very clearly into my spirit! "You have not, because you ask not!" It was a huge revelation to me and something that I speak about often in my ministry! We need to ask for the opportunity to participate! God is waiting for us to enter in. He is a gentleman; He will never force His will on us, ever! Prior to our next communion service, I asked for the opportunity to sing my song and was welcomed to do so. As I began to sing, the doors of the sanctuary opened and over two hundred youth, from the youth service, quietly entered and surrounded the hundreds already seated. The impact of the generations coming together moved many of us to tears. ***How Beautiful.***

How beautiful the tender eyes
That choose to forgive and never despise
How beautiful, how beautiful,
how beautiful is the body of Christ

And as He lay down His life
We offer this sacrifice
That we will live just as He died
Willing to pay the price
Willing to pay the price

It was a profoundly moving tribute to the body of Christ gathering in unity. A clear vision continues to resonate deep inside me as witness to the ministry calling on our lives, to build unity among the generations and denominations today. It is also such a beautiful reminder of how God healed my heart and replaced judgement and offense with appreciation and honor.

I also learned to 'ask' that God would enlarge my territory with more opportunities to serve by reciting the prayers I'd found other's prayed in the scriptures. Many of the frontlines warriors we meet today were also repeating and meditating on The Jabez Prayer. It says in – **"Jabez prayed to the God of Israel saying, "Oh that You would bless me indeed and enlarge my border, and that Your hand might be with me, and that You would keep me from harm that it may not pain me!"** It concludes by saying, **And God granted him what he requested."** (1Chronicles 4:10 – KJV) If God could do it for Jabez, He could open more doors for me too. LOL! If you want to do what God needs you to do...... just ask, seek and knock!

"Ask, Seek, Knock"became a mantra for me in ministry. As God showed me another song to sing or another way I could use my time and talents for Him, I would ask for the opportunity, offer my services and extend my hand. Through the years that have followed, if a ministry opportunity presented itself somewhere away from home, I would "ask, seek and knock" looking for additional opportunities in the area. Hundreds of phone calls and emails later, ministry tours were created because I asked, seldom waiting for an unsolicited invitation.

After years of calling and traveling, I was really tired and crying out to the Lord one late night between High Prairie and Rocky Mountain House, Alberta. Admittedly, I was pretty much begging Him for permission to stop asking! In fact, trying to stay awake at the wheel, I was loudly bargaining with God, saying, "How about we just stop with the asking thing Lord?! How about we just stop and spend time at home, waiting for the phone to ring? I would much rather be visiting the kids and grandchildren more. Please God? I'm so tired!" Pulling off to the side of the road, I fell asleep for a few hours. Upon awakening, I felt pretty sure I was done with the whole ministry life and having to 'ask' for opportunities to serve!

Later that afternoon at my girlfriend's place, I was getting a tour of their lovely home. Betty McKay Blackwell was showing me the lovely stepping stones she made! They were incredibly beautiful, simple and yet insightful. Suddenly, she pulled one out and said it was an interesting one. It was much more detailed than what she and her granddaughter would usually make. Betty actually commented that she wasn't sure why she'd written out the whole scripture on the rock as it was completely opposite to their usual design strategy. As I looked at it more closely, I smiled and said, "Well, that's because it's probably the most important verse in the whole world!" Oh yeah, right before my eyes was the entire verse I'd been discussing with God just the night before! LOL! **"Ask, and it will be given to you; seek, and you will find; knock, and it will be opened to you."** (Matthew 7:7 – KJV). A gentle peace came over me as Betty began to laugh! She said, "I knew I must be making it for someone, but I had *no* idea who! Here you go! God obviously wants you to have it!" The stepping stone still sits right outside of our main entrance at home. It is a gentle reminder that He has taught me a few things he expects me to remember and share! I have been reminded of God's strategies for successful ministry living through the writing of this book. I 'ask' once more, right here, right now:

> For prayer warriors to pray!
> For invitations to sing and speak.
> For financial support and sponsors to give.
> For corporate advertisers to partner with us.
> For the opportunity to share my prophetic worship anointing.

For an entire tribe to rise with me to "be the change we want to see in the world!"

WHEN THE JOURNEY IS HARD AND THERE ARE
MOUNTAINS TO CLIMB...
YOU JUST SPEND YOUR RETIREMENT FUND! LOL! J<><

Every once in a while I'm reminded about that tree I saw in heaven and how one day we'd understand everything that did or didn't come to pass in our ministry. The lack of money had begun limiting our ministry and so, on a deep and personal level, I began praying about what to do. God reminded us that financial support from Him would generally come through the giving of others. In a few very important ways He also showed us clearly how His plans for us have been cut off. Pastors told us they couldn't afford to have their parishioners give money to outside causes or itinerant ministers during the feared economic future they were facing. As much as they loved us and appreciated our ministry, we couldn't minister with them anymore. Others removed us from their bulletin announcements and prayer chains and decided we would no longer be allowed to give ministry reports or request support.

A gentleman came up to Bob and me after we'd shared a ministry report at his church. He told us that he'd realized while we were speaking that he'd forgotten to send us money. We laughed together. He explained how he remembered reading our newsletter and how the Holy Spirit had prompted him to support us. "Until today", he said, "I totally forgot about it". Rather sheepishly, he apologized and asked how we were doing. He asked how the past project had gone. We explained that it hadn't! We wondered as we left that day if God was finally going to let that original vision be fulfilled! Excited, we waited, but nothing ever came...

During the winter of 2014, I made the decision to sell my house in Arizona. It was supposed to be my retirement fund but instead, I chose to sell it and pay off the line of credit and the expenses attached to each of our outstanding projects. What if God's plan for us reaching the world, means I'm not allowed to store up my wealth for my unknown future? This entire ministry began with God speaking directly into Bob's heart about the **Cost of a Soul**. Obviously, nothing has changed! Although Bob and I are feeling much older and could be more discouraged than ever before, I laugh out loud as I'm reminded this life we live is called a 'battlefield'!

Still on Jude's hard drive at Alone Stone in NS are nearly enough tunes to finish another album. **TRIBUTE! Songs of Faith, Freedom and Family** will be a tribute to our nation, love and life! We will honor our veterans with *A Soldiers Lament* and the recitation, *A Veteran Died Today*. Our Full Gospel Businessmen's roots will be celebrated with Karen Vanderwell's beautiful song **Canada** in a mix called *Dominion Medley* – a powerful declaration of God's majesty and dominion over the land we call home and a very important song! Royalties need paid and CD's need manufactured, etc. but we've already invested a good bit into it and have felt God telling us to get it done and so we will.

Interestingly, finances did not come in for the book project either! Meeting Charlotte was ordained by God and we know it! Writing this book, entirely His plan too, as coincidences are not part of God's vocabulary. The best part of this 'book' project has been how God has reminded me of His call on my life, one I need to be reminded of even today. Selling the house means the book has been done also – the proof is in your hands! LOL! : ()

The Christmas show, **Light in the Darkness,** was made for television and requires thousands more dollars on top of the $16,000 already invested in order to get it to air. The great news is that as the royalties and synchronization fees are paid, we will be allowed to air it on TV and the Internet for seven years!

Destiny and Her Happy Sword will be further developed. More characters have been added to the story. Jasmine is the Holy Spirit, a little blue bird that flutters around and speaks while on Destiny's shoulder. A rodeo-riding, lassoing cowboy named Zach and a ninja warrior named Caleb are successfully fighting the evil forces in our world, too. The characters carry the names of my children and the visions often overwhelm me and bring me to tears. A blond, spiky-haired Debra is under the tree offering advice, wisdom and encouragement, and another character is the Majestic One, overseeing the world from a place of light and peace. The whole story is about childlike faith. Even though it is being done in animated fashion to appeal to children, the message will be totally applicable to adults as well. The Kingdom of God, through their positive message, *will* take back all authority in four of the seven mountains discussed earlier: Family, Business, Arts and Entertainment, as well as the Media Mountains! Amen? Amen! As Christians we are not supposed to be living mediocre lives, but fighting valiantly to destroy the demons and things that so easily distract us. **Destiny and the Happy Sword** will be used by the Lord to help open eyes and ears! Today it is just another powerful dream for ministry, but I believe one day soon we'll be able to finish these cartoons and watch Destiny change the lives of children and adults the world over!

I have committed to the continued financial support of our television and Internet ministries BUT will fight the feelings of discouragement and defeat with a spirit of expectation and belief for partners and investors to join us on the frontline, sooner instead of later! Our home church, and Pastors Moe and Anita Palmier are the only ones who have remained faithful to this commitment. When I was praying for $150 (US funds) in order to secure our XPMedia channel on a monthly basis – God told me to call our first sponsor. Not only did this busy, hardworking man actually answer his phone which I felt was an actual miracle to me, but Wilfred Smith immediately committed one hundred dollars per month. I wept. The next day, the Palmiers and 'our home church, 'People of Praise', committed another $200 monthly. Brother Wilf has since gone on to glory but oh, the confirmation and encouragement I received as these two partners joined us.

Is There A God? Hell, Yeah! J<><

Literally just days before the contract for publishing this autobiography was signed, God changed the name of the book from "The Jodi Faith Story, LOL!" to its present title. Not a big surprise as I had been sensing a shift was going to happen, but I still laugh out loud considering how God introduced me to the new title! Years ago, my heart was heavy with the news that atheists purchased millions of dollars in advertising. On buses and billboards all over the world they were broadcasting their view. 'There is probably no god, so relax and enjoy life!' the advertisements said. I began praying and asking God what we could do. Together Bob and I began facilitating round table discussion groups and sharing videos that spoke to the truth of creation (Lou Giglio) and the fact that the Bible is proven to be true. ***Recommended reading: Surprised by Faith by Dr. Don Bierle.*** These discussion groups were titled, Is There A God, Hell, Yeah!

One evening while praying about this global campaign and how we could help, I received a powerful vision. I *was in a diner… the waitress was pouring me a cup of coffee as we looked out the window and saw a bus going by with the message glaring loudly before us! The waitress was horrified as she looked at me. Tears forming in her eyes, she desperately said to me, "If there isn't a God, what am I going to do?" In the vision I began singing a song of hope to her. Almost like I imagined Jesus in the temple, I saw myself rising up and turning tables upside down as I made a righteous stand, as if to say, don't tell me my God doesn't exist! The song rising up in me was a declaration… I sang of the truth of God in my world, alive and well in the situations and circumstances of my life! The final scene of the vision was revealed. I entered the diner with a group of vigilant Christ followers. The transformation was evident – where darkness and hopelessness had been, light and hope could be felt! The entire atmosphere had changed! The waitress had received the truth that had set her free. Together we began to celebrate as another city bus went past the window. This time, on the side of the bus, was a new ad campaign and I was standing triumphantly, declaring loudly, "Is there a God? Hell, Yeah!!"*

A great title and a great truth! Hopefully lessons *have* been learned through the stories Bob and I have shared with you. Out of our brokenness, God has brought us to a place of complete restoration! If you look at what Jesus did in us and to us and now through us, you *can* choose to believe in a God who restores! Our story is about second chances! It seems the survival of Bob's and my marriage is Satan's continual challenge but he'll give up as we persevere together for the cause of Christ. God showed me that we were destined to be together in the beginning and I choose to honor that! There is fall-out from the past which we are dealing with even today.

Our "blended family" situation has not always been easy and we continue to pray for protection of the relationships we have with our children and healing of the hurts we've inflicted and experienced. In spite of the difficult challenges, we've often come away blessed by the camaraderie and love shared during a family visit. Bob and I enjoy being able to travel and spend time with our children and grandchildren. Each of our children has excelled and thrived in building successful careers and beautiful families. In spring 2014, we have twenty grandchildren! LOL! Babysitting thrills our hearts and is often beneficial if we visit and can be of help with child minding, etc. The relationships we enjoy are so special! We are grateful that the Lord has blessed our family in wonderful ways! We love being able to testify that through Christ 'Blended Family Bliss' *is* possible!" LOL!

Bob and I believe God can completely turn difficult situations around and we are living proof of that! 'Beauty from Ashes!' I am a living sign and a wonder! From hopeless and homeless to living the abundant life and fulfilling my destiny with joy unspeakable! From drinking 40 ounces of scotch on a weekend and smoking a bag of pot a week to being a drug-free living speaker in schools is remarkable! From being forbidden from singing for seventeen years in my first marriage to having my songs played in over fifty countries on radio and singing to the nations of the world is nothing short of miraculous! As a once-broken young woman who found her voice, our entire ministry began because my husband encouraged me to use the gifts God had given me. Thank you, Jesus, for Bob's wisdom and discernment. As the Canadian 2013 Female Vocalist of the Year you're obviously NOT done with this 'Lady of Destiny' quite yet! Hallelujah! In His Word, God promises to make good out of even the worst of circumstances, and He has. In the Bible it says that God restores the years stolen from us! The accelerated music and media career I have enjoyed is perfect proof of exactly that! Only ten years of ministry and God has taken us to the nations. Another great verses says, **"And we know that all that happens to us is working for our good if we love God and are fitting into his plans."** Romans 8:28 (TLB). Although I couldn't have imagined anything good coming out of my situation as I laid in the dirt back in 1994, the testimonies we share impact the lives of others on a daily basis!

As this book was being completed, Bob and I were in Winnipeg. I asked my cousin, Martha Peters Stewart, who is a voracious reader, whether she might be willing to 'proofread' the book. She looked at me with a huge smile and said, "No, but I know someone who might!" She had been at a women's convention just the week before. She had visited with and gotten to know a wonderful new friend who felt called to help 'proof-read' the stories being written by people like myself! LOL! Not only were Bob and me able to meet with her the next week, but today I know more about prepositions, split infinitives and possessives before gerunds (Sorry Jacqueline Chartrand, I'm still not sure what that means?) then I ever imagined or thought possible! LOL! After we spent an entire week on one last edit, which she made us do by reading the entire book aloud, I was so grateful for the time spent! My life is so busy it was miraculous that God had blocked an entire week where I was available! Jacqueline was almost shocked to discover that not only was I willing to spend the time, but that I want to bring excellence to everything I dedicate to my Lord and would have been horrified to have let it go to the publisher the way it was. Is there a God, oh, yeah, and He obviously cares about you, the reader, not being distracted by my poor grammar being replaced with something more acceptable so 'the small stuff!' Haha!

My healing journey began with Christian counseling and has continued through the years as God has introduced us to important mentors and teachers. As we moved forward in greater authority, God allowed Bob and me to minister with Joan Hunter for one short week one summer.

Our marriage shifted as she taught us how to be released from old blood covenants formed through sexual relationships. Our ministry and our lives were forever changed by the wisdom we received from Joan's ministry of hope and healing. The prayers she teaches are great strategies for dealing with life. Her *Healing The Whole Man Handbook* is an insightful resource for anyone wanting to live a victorious life! The following is just one example of how she taught us to pray personally and in ministry for others!

*"**Cast Our Cares On The Altar** Father, I am carrying the burdens of my relationships and circumstances. I choose to lay all my cares, all my worries, all my fears, all things I cannot change on Your altar. Father, I lay my spouse on Your altar. Father, I lay my children on Your altar. Father, I lay my job, my finances on Your altar. Father I lay (name of circumstances that you cannot change) on Your altar. You are my supply and You alone can move in my circumstances. I give these to You and trust You with them, in Jesus' name."*

God wants us to be free from the things that burden us so that we can move into everything He has for us! Joan's healing schools and books highlight the ministry she shared with her parents, Charles and Frances Hunter. They are full of healing prayers, revelation and understanding. They have become part of our arsenal of weapons on the frontline! We encourage you to plug into the Joan Hunter ministry, too.

Bob and I know that not everyone who reads this book understands the truth of God's existence, His love or His awesome and marvellous plan for their lives. As I said at the beginning of this book, there were many years when I tried to ignore the existence of God in my life, but He continued to pursue me, love me and quite frankly, fight for me! Is there a God? Oh, yeah! From that very first time when I heard His audible voice in the midst of the worst time of my life, I knew He was real and engaged in my life on a deep and personal level. Over and over He made Himself real to me. Ask and He will make himself available and real to you, too!

In Matthew 13 verses 49 and 50, it says **"This is how it will be at the end of the age. The angels will come and separate the wicked from the righteous and throw them into the blazing furnace, where there will be weeping and gnashing of teeth."** Jesus Himself spoke of hell. He said He came to seek and save the lost. A friend of my dad, Dr. Hoogeveen, wrote a book called, **Tell Me Doc, Will I Live Forever?** It chronicled the journey of many patients who died and experienced horrific visits to hell before being revived. Coming back to earth, they said they knew that Jesus would save them. And save them He did! On the Internet today people are sharing testimony after testimony of experiencing hell. In Hebrews 7:25 it says – **"Therefore He (Jesus) is able, once and forever, to save those who come to God through Him. He lives forever to intercede with God on our behalf."**

And we need to be saved! Satan is real and has set up the demonic realm as all-powerful in the world we live in! Satan had been an angel who became jealous of Jesus and was cast out of Heaven. Called the thief, his entire mandate is to "steal, kill and destroy!" This could be an entirely new book, LOL! I believe he knew I would be dangerous for the Kingdom of God and so he set out to *steal* my destiny purposes from me. The truth is Satan wants to *steal* God's love from each of us. He wants to *kill* our God-ordained dreams and purposes and leave us *destroyed*, chewed up and spit out by life, incapable of living the abundant joy-filled existence God intended for us! Hopelessness and fear are making themselves known in the highways and byways as Satan is aggressively hunting the lost. From the evil and vampires and endless darkness being portrayed on TV to the high rate of teenage suicide, crime, drug abuse and sexual perversion, the demonic realm has become more and more apparent in our world. A recent video in a hospital emergency room shows a demon walking above the patient in the bed. See http://www.tribulation-now.org/3685-2/. The commentary says: "*The dimensions are merging at this time. This is a warning that the Great Tribulation is about to start at any time. The demonic realm is merging with our dimension NOW. This picture was taken from a security camera located in a hospital intensive care ward. Here you see a filthy demon coming to take the soul of the person in the bed. If you are living in willful, habitual and unrepentant sin even if you believe in Jesus you are not going to make it. The Gate is NARROW.*"

Jim Isakson, of Life Ministries in Colorado, shares his personal testimony of growing up in the church and knowing Jesus and how during a bout of meningitis was shown hell. People remember him telling his story. He experienced a sense of falling into great darkness and being enfolded in such deep despair, that it rocked his world and changed his life. Satan knows there is a hell! He knows he himself will be damned and he is intent on taking as many souls with him as he can! Why? I believe it's because he knows nothing grieves the heart of God more than the lost soul, unrepentant and rebelliously denying His power and purposes in their lives! God made each one of us with a *void* that only He can fill. He also loved us enough to give us the opportunity of free will. The Word of God says, **"It is not His will that even one soul should perish!"** (2 Peter 3:9) That is why He sent His Son Jesus to die for us though. Christ died for every accidental or intentional sin mankind could come up with! A perfectly timed plan, so that, as believers, we can stand before the judgment of God Almighty, completely faultless. Through the blood atonement Jesus offers, our sins are washed away! We can live in absolute freedom and authority! What an awesome gift! Not just here on earth, but most importantly, throughout all eternity. God's ultimate plan is for us to share Heaven with Him forever! In John 3:16, the Bible states: **"For God so loved the world that He gave his only Son, that whosoever believes in Him shall not perish, but have everlasting life!"**

The story is simple. God sent his son for heaven as a babe in the Christmas manger. He allowed His son Jesus, who lived a sinless life as teacher and prophet, to die on the cross of Calvary for the sin and rebellion of mankind. Completely separated from God, Jesus himself visited hell. Overcoming sin, the Bible says, He took back the keys of death and pain and victoriously He rose from the grave! Eyewitness accounts have lived on through the generations of how Jesus, alive and restored after death, visited His disciples! Then, Jesus needed to leave earth in order for the Holy Spirit to come and dwell in us, empowering us with that same resurrection power.

Bob loves the story of a wonderful old saint by the name of Mr. Genor from George Street in Australia! He was radically "saved" one day and his life was miraculously, remarkably changed by experiencing God's saving grace! He committed his life to asking one simple question, at least ten times a day, of the people he met on the street corner. "Tell me sir/madam, are you saved?" He would ask, "If you should die tonight, would you go to Heaven?" Jesus is the only way to God. Have you accepted the gift of salvation offered by God's only Son, Jesus Christ? We will stand before God and have to answer this question! In fact, in Revelation 20:15 the Bible says that unless our name is written in the Book of Life we will be cast into the "Lake of Fire." Forgiveness is our ticket out of eternal damnation. Simply say, "Yes! God, forgive me!" and you too will be saved. Jesus will walk alongside you and the Holy Spirit *will* be with you.

Bob's favorite verse is Ephesians 2:8–9 (KJV). **"For it is by grace you have been saved, through faith—and this is not from yourselves, it is the gift of God— not by works, so that no one can boast."** Bob always says it makes so much more sense, than thinking we can get ourselves to heaven through anything we might do! It's all about God's grace extended! I love the same verse in The Message version, which starting in verse 7 says: **"Now, God has us where He wants us, with all the time in this world and the next to shower grace and kindness upon us in Christ**

Jesus. Saving is all His idea, and all His work. All we do is trust him enough to let Him do it. It's God's gift from start to finish! We don't play the major role. If we did, we'd probably go around bragging that we'd done the whole thing! No, we neither make, nor save ourselves. God does both the making and saving. He creates each of us by Christ Jesus to join Him in the work He does, the good work He has gotten ready for us to do, work we had better be doing."

UNTIL WE MEET AGAIN HE HAS WORK FOR US TO DO!
EMPOWERMENT RECEIVED AND DESTINY
PURPOSES FULFILLED! J<><

Bob and I are learning about the truth of Heaven from 4 year-old boys and 32 year-old men and from Kat Kerr! You've got to check her out online! For ten years God has taken her to visit heaven so *we* can know what to expect once we get there! It's absolutely tremendous! We always like to suggest we have good news and bad news when singing some of the old heaven songs like **When The Roll Is Called Up Yonder!** The good news being the fact that we'll be spending eternity together with you BUT the bad news is that we're not dead yet! LOL!

Indifference and apathy are huge issues in the lives of fundamental Christians today. We are called to rise up and be advocates for good. God wants us to be completely, wonderfully immersed in living life to the full! He wants us to be living, breathing examples of the overcoming spirit and the grace and mercy of God! He didn't send His Son, Jesus, so we could live a mediocre life! No! God's plan for us includes victorious, triumphant life! He has given us absolute authority as a royal priesthood. We need to figure out who we are in Christ in order to walk in the full authority He has given us!

Where God is love, mercy and justice, the world sees Him and His people as angry, ugly, intolerant and most sadly, indifferent. Whether you agree or not, I believe Satan and his army have done a pretty good job of turning the tables on the reputation of God and His people. At a time when more and more people are feeling overwhelmed and without hope, Bob and I have often heard that the last place people feel they can go is to the Christian church. Perhaps this is because of the ways they have been hurt by organized religion. I believe it may also be because Satan has *stolen* a good reputation from

Christianity. So often humanity has made excuses for its behavior instead of repenting and turning from its wicked ways. 'Integrity' is not the first word most people will use when describing the church today! From James 3:17-18 (MSG) we pray, **"Real wisdom, God's wisdom, begins with a holy life and is characterized by getting along with others. It is gentle and reasonable, overflowing with mercy and blessings, not hot one day and cold the next, not two-faced. You can develop a healthy, robust community that lives right with God and enjoy its results *only* if you do the hard work of getting along with each other and treating each other with dignity and honor."**

Before Jesus came it was a time of visitation. God could only visit His servants empowering them so they could get the job at hand done then He was gone. He could not dwell within them. We now live in a time of habitation! He will never leave us or forsake us! God with us! We can overcome every obstacle, empowered by the strength of Christ in us! As we ask Jesus to enter into our lives, we enter into God's blessed realm. The rebuke and reality of being separated from God are removed from us and the promises flow. After He died and rose from the dead, Jesus visited His followers. Although a few of them had seen Him and believed He had risen from the grave (as He'd shown them the holes in his hands) the eyewitness account in Mark 16:14-20 (MSG) reports – **"As the eleven were eating supper, He appeared and took them to task most severely for their stubborn unbelief, refusing to believe those who had seen Him raised up. Then He said, "Go into the world. Go everywhere and announce the Message of God's Good News to one and all. Whoever believes and is baptized is saved; whoever refuses to believe is damned."** (I'm interjecting here to say that if Jesus said I'm damned if I don't believe, it's good enough for me!)

Continuing at verse 17 it says: **"These are some of the signs that will accompany believers: They will throw out demons in my name, they will speak in new tongues, they will take snakes in their hands, they will drink poison and not be hurt, they will lay hands on the sick and make them well.**

"Then the Master Jesus, after briefing them, was taken up to heaven, and He sat down beside God in the place of honor. And the disciples went everywhere preaching, the Master working right with them, validating the Message with indisputable evidence."

The eyewitness accounts of the miracles Jesus did have lived on over 2000 years. He is well known as a prophet and teacher but the Bible has been proven historically correct. All it takes is to walk the land where He walked to see the legend lives on in truth and justice! Scripture has been preserved for the generations. The miracles He did will be done by Christ followers the world over until He comes again! God has so much in store for each of us and we look forward to continuing to share the stories of how He continues to show up faithful in our lives and yours too!

In the Bible it also says, "We will do more than Christ did!" In John 14(MSG) 11-14 it says, **"Believe me: I am in my Father and my Father is in me. If you can't believe that, believe what you see—these works. The person who trusts me will not only do what I'm doing, but even greater things, because I, on my way to the Father, am giving you the same work to do that I've been doing. You can count on it. From now on, whatever you request along the lines of who I am and what I am doing, I'll do it. That's how the Father will be seen for who He is in the Son. I mean it. Whatever you request in this way, I'll do."**

So, Lord, I pray for courage and peace as I move into an entirely new area of influence and authority! We've been feeling somewhat defeated but believe You have opened the door to something completely new! Since I still haven't heard back from **Dragon's Den**, where I auditioned for investor funding in order to grow our ministry and change the world, I will now move into the marketplace. *Father, I ask that you will protect me from any potential distractions and keep me focused on Your will every day as I begin the climb toward the pinnicle of the BUSINESS MOUNTAIN!!. I pray You will help me grow in influence for the Kingdom's sake as I follow your leading during the upcoming journey!* All our 'Princess Parties' and 'Girlfriend and Giggles' events will be sponsored by Work For Widows©, Jamberries©, and Rodan and Fields© (R+F). As they launch their skin-care line in Canada, I will begin to build a business that will generate income and allow us to complete the work we are called to in ministry. *Thank-you in advance for all you're going to do in me and through me and too me during this next season! I'm excited!! Thank-you for the encouragement I've received from Bob! Thank-you for removing so much of the strife we were experiences because of unmet expectations, finances and support!! Bless Bob too as he is able to rest just a bit* *more... Playing Bridge weekly and playing ball! What a blessing it was for him to umpire and coach Little League last season!*

God has shown me in so many ways that this step into business is his will! Telling the tale will probably be the next book – but it's been with fear and trepidation that I've taken each step! LOL! Ironically, I laid down the music ministry so I could concentrate on business, booked a cross-Canada pre-launch tour and trip to Atlanta, Georgia with R+F on Bob's Aerogold© air-miles and then, drum-roll please, was invited to sing at the R+F International Convention in Atlanta on September 11-13th, 2014! LOL! I can see a whole bunch of my new Rodan and Fields friends singing *Lady of Destiny* all over the continent!

Wherever you go, whatever God has for you, let's agree it will be used by Him for His Glory!! Please pray the same for us, too! We choose a final blessing from scripture again. We decree and declare over us all, from Isaiah 60, for such a time as this! *Arise, Shine!*

Arise, shine, for your light has come, arise shine
Arise, shine, for your light has come
And the Glory of the Lord rises upon you
And the Glory of the Lord rises upon you

Matthew 5:14-16 – **Who is the Light of the World?** *You are the light of the world.* **Let your light shine before men in such a way that they may see your good works, and glorify your Father who is in Heaven. Love, J**<><

The following songs are mentioned in these writings – Jodi invites you to "purchase" the entire 4 album set at a wonderfully discounted rate (4 albums for $50.00) as a "preferred partner" upon purchasing or receiving this book.

Use promo code – Partner – Order at www.bobandjodifaith.com or at our online store thru www.xpmedia.com/channel/bobandjodifaith

Page 2 *"An Eagle When She Flies"* Album – Hands United
Page 10 *"He's Everything To Me!"* Album – Tribute
Page 11 *"I Have A Dream"* Album – Hands United
Page 35 *"Circle of Friends"* Album – Hands United
Page 44 *"Love Can Build A Bridge"* Album – Hands United
Page 47 *"I Know Who Holds Tomorrow"* Album – Now Is The Time
Page 65 *"How Beautiful"* Album – Tribute
Page 67 *"Broken Love"* DVD – Light In The Darkness (LITD)
Page 85 *"The Potter's Hand"* Album – Second Chance
Page 86 *"Only God Could Love You More"* Album – Tribute
Page 107 *"Bethlehem Star"* DVD – LITD
Page 108 *"Jesus You Are Him"* DVD – LITD
Page 116 *"Second Chance"* Album – Second Chance
Page 120 *"Red Coat Trail"* Album – Now Is The Time
Page 120 *"Walkin' On The Water"* Album – Now Is The Time
Page 127 *"Cost of A Soul"* Album – Second Chance
Page 145 *"Lady of Destiny"* Album – Now Is The Time
Page 151 *"Random Acts of Kindness"* Album – Now Is The Time
Page 171 *"I Am There"* Album – Now Is The Time; DVD – LITD; Hands United
Page 191 *"Hands United"* Album – Hands United
Page 198 *"CLEAN"* – www.xpmedia.com/channel/bobandjodifaith
Page 201 *"Grandmas"* Album – Hands United; Tribute
Page 206 *"How Beautiful"* Album – Tribute
Page 224 *"Arise Shine"* Album – Hands United

Recommended Reading – The Bible is quoted through-out from any of the following versions:

The Message (MSG) Copyright © 1993, 1994, 1995, 1996, 2000, 2001, 2002 by Eugene H. Peterson

Living Bible (TLB) The Living Bible copyright © 1971 by Tyndale House Foundation. Used by permission of Tyndale House Publishers Inc., Carol Stream, Illinois 60188. All rights reserved.

New International Version (NIV) Holy Bible, New International Version®, NIV® Copyright © 1973, 1978, 1984, 2011 by Biblica, Inc.® Used by permission. All rights reserved worldwide.

King James Version (KJV) by Public Domain

Additional recommended reading -
Page 31 "The Blessing" by Gary Smalley and John Trent
Page 31 "The Five Love Languages" by Gary Chapman.
Page 69 "The Bait Of Satan" by John Bevere.
Page 213 "Surprised by Faith" by Don Bierle
Page 215 "Healing the Whole Man Handbook" by Joan Hunter
Page 217 "Tell Me, Doc, Will I Live Forever" by Dr. Hoogeveen

Recommended Ministries
Page 34 – Stonecroft Ministries; See www.stonecroft.org
Page 153 – Work For Widows; See www.workforwidows.com
Page 158 – End-time Handmaidens and Servants; See www.eth-s.org
Page 161 – Reinhard Bonnke and Christ For All Nations. See www.cfan.org
Page 165 – Patricia King; See www.patriciakingministries.org
Page 166 – LaRed; www.lared.org
Page 166 – Global Priority; www.globalpriority.org
Page 166 – Lance Wallnau; www.lancewallnau.com
Page 166 – XP Media; www.xpmedia.com
Page 213 – Don Bierle of Faith Search International; www.faith-search.org
Page 213 – Lou Giglio – www.NESTLearning.com/Louie_Giglio
Page 215 – Joan Hunter Ministries; www.joanhunter.org
Page 218 – Jim Isakson of New Life Ministries – To Hell and Back – https://www.youtube.com/watch?v=FTajYZJDnQk

For additional information, please call 403-580-6066;
Email at bobandjodifaith@gmail.com
Mail – PO Box 296; Lafleche, Sask. Can.SOH 2KO

Your partnership in our ministry is a wonderful blessing.
Donate online at www.bobandjodifaith.com
or mail your gifts to "People of Praise" PO Box
208, Lafleche, Sask. SOH 2KO

Printed in Canada